Your Personal Horoscope 2017

♑

Capricorn

Your Personal Horoscope 2017

♑

Capricorn

22nd December–20th January

igloobooks

igloobooks

Published in 2016
by Igloo Books Ltd
Cottage Farm
Sywell
NN6 0BJ
www.igloobooks.com

Produced for Igloo Books by Foulsham Publishing Ltd, The Old Barrel Store, Drayman's Lane, Marlow, Bucks SL7 2FF, England

FIR003 0716
2 4 6 8 10 9 7 5 3 1
ISBN: 978-1-78557-506-8

This is an abridged version of material originally published in Old Moore's Horoscope and Astral Diary.

Cover images: iStock
Cover designed by Nicholas Gage

Printed and manufactured in China

CONTENTS

INTRODUCTION

Your Personal Horoscopes have been specifically created to allow you to get the most from astrological patterns and the way they have a bearing on not only your zodiac sign, but nuances within it. Using the diary section of the book you can read about the influences and possibilities of each and every day of the year. It will be possible for you to see when you are likely to be cheerful and happy or those times when your nature is in retreat and you will be more circumspect. The diary will help to give you a feel for the specific 'cycles' of astrology and the way they can subtly change your day-to-day life. For example, when you see the sign ☿, this means that the planet Mercury is retrograde at that time. Retrograde means it appears to be running backwards through the zodiac. Such a happening has a significant effect on communication skills, but this is only one small aspect of how the Personal Horoscope can help you.

With Your Personal Horoscope the story doesn't end with the diary pages. It includes simple ways for you to work out the zodiac sign the Moon occupied at the time of your birth, and what this means for your personality. In addition, if you know the time of day you were born, it is possible to discover your Ascendant, yet another important guide to your personal make-up and potential.

Many readers are interested in relationships and in knowing how well they get on with people of other astrological signs. You might also be interested in the way you appear to very different sorts of individuals. If you are such a person, the section on Venus will be of particular interest. Despite the rapidly changing position of this planet, you can work out your Venus sign, and learn what bearing it will have on your life.

Using Your Personal Horoscope you can travel on one of the most fascinating and rewarding journeys that anyone can take – the journey to a better realisation of self.

THE ESSENCE OF CAPRICORN

Exploring the Personality of Capricorn the Goat

(22ND DECEMBER–20TH JANUARY)

What's in a sign?

You probably think of yourself as being the least complicated person to be found anywhere. Although this is basically true, that doesn't necessarily mean that everyone understands you quite as well as they might. When faced with the real world you are practical, capable and resourceful. That means that you get on well with whatever needs to be done. Where you might sometimes fall down is in terms of communicating your intentions to the world at large – mostly it doesn't seem all that important to do so. In other words, you are not the world's best talker, and probably don't even want to be.

When it comes to sweeping away the red tape and actually getting down to the task in hand, you are second to none. Dextrous and adaptable in all matters that need your unique logic, you come at all problems with the same determination to sort them out. However, your ruling planet is cold, ponderous Saturn, and that could be where the potential problems start. Although you have a kind heart and a genuine desire to improve the lot of others, your methods are sometimes misunderstood. Some people might think you a little aloof, or even difficult to talk to. You have frequent quiet spells and often seem to be particularly content with your own company. On rare occasions this can leave you isolated.

Sharing what you are with the world at large is the most important factor on the road to a more contented life, though even this isn't certain, because most Capricorn people tend to be fairly happy with being the way they are. All the same, when those around you want to see something actually being done, they will call on you. Success is not hard for you to achieve, particularly in a career sense. You don't mind getting your hands dirty and can usually be relied upon to find ingenious answers when they are most needed.

In matters of love you are sincere and will work long and hard for your family. Romantically speaking you take some time to get going but can be ardent and sincere when you finally do. Routines don't bother you, and you can also learn to be adaptable.

Capricorn resources

You probably don't think of yourself as being the most dynamic person in the world, though you certainly are one of the most capable. When others are looking for answers, even in very practical matters, you are in there sorting things out. It's the nuts and bolts of the world that are most important, and you don't seem to have too much trouble fixing broken things – whether it's the living room chair, or the heart of a dear friend.

Instead of trying to be one of life's exciting go-getters, you are likely to be more comfortable working slowly and steadily, sometimes in the background. But this doesn't mean that you fail to make a positive impression. On the contrary, you are very necessary to those who form a part of your life, and they are ever aware of the important part you play. It isn't given to everyone to be showy and flashy, and in any case even if you forced yourself down such roads you probably wouldn't be at all comfortable in a role that doesn't come naturally to you.

One of your greatest attributes is your dry sense of humour. It's always possible for you to make others laugh, even during the most awkward or difficult situations. When the world looks particularly dark we all need a Capricorn subject along to lighten the load. You make a good colleague, know well how to co-operate and tend to work capably, either as part of a team, or when circumstances dictate, on your own.

Your greatest resource, and the one that has made many Capricorn people famous over the years, is your capacity to keep going. When there is a problem to be solved, a bridge to build, or a family to support under difficult circumstances, you really come into your own. This is probably because you don't understand the meaning of the word failure. You can find ways round any number of obstacles, and remain dependable, even when the world and his dog are falling to pieces. Add to this the fact that you are consistent and reliable and it shouldn't be too hard for you to enjoy being a capable Capricorn.

Beneath the surface

Although you might not appear to be very complicated when viewed from the perspective of those who see you on a daily basis, you are actually very complex. The reason that this is not obvious lies in the fact that you betray very little of your inner mind in your day-to-day interactions with others. In the main they see you as being capable and settled – but how wrong they can be.

The fact is that you are rarely totally sure of yourself. The confidence to get things done disguises how often you shake inside, and especially so if you are forced into the public arena. You probably wouldn't relish having to do any sort of presentation or to be put on the spot in front of individuals you consider to be more dynamic than you are. Despite this there are strong saving graces. Even when times are tough, or when you do feel a little shaky inside, your natural way forward is to keep plugging away. In some respects your zodiac sign may represent one of the bravest of them all. You won't allow yourself to be bettered by anyone, and the more pressure that is put upon you to fail, the greater is your internal desire for success.

In matters of emotion you are complicated and difficult to understand. You view relationships with the same patience that you bring to almost all facets of life. Friends can misuse or even abuse you for a while, but there is a breaking point within Capricorn that appears sudden, and very final. And once you have made up your mind to a particular course of action, there isn't any force in the world that will prevent you from implementing it.

Your natural planetary ruler is Saturn, the Lord of Time. As a result you are inclined to see things in the medium and longer term. You rarely show yourself to be impatient and carefully choose a course of action, using mental processes that usually follow tried and tested paths. You won't be hurried or pushed and will always stick to methods of working that seem to have worked for you in the past. Although this might sometimes make you feel lacking in colour or variety, you almost always get where you want to go. Occasionally your inner mind takes a great leap in logic. This can lead to a sudden change in attitude and actions that will shock the world. And why not? Even Capricorns need to keep people guessing sometimes.

You may not be the easiest person in the world to understand, or to get to know fully. Don't worry. The inner secrecy of your nature is half your appeal.

Making the best of yourself

We all need to realise what makes us tick, and to come to terms with the most comfortable way in which we can react with the world at large. This is just as true for the zodiac sign of Capricorn as it is for any other. But nobody is perfect, so what can you do to use your skills to the full and to get on better with those who share the planet with you?

Well for starters, it wouldn't be a bad idea to let others know what you are doing – and why. In practical situations especially it's sometimes much easier for you simply to get on and finish a task on your own. And despite your capabilities this is probably why you are not the world's best teacher. It's simply less complicated to get something done, and then to move on patiently to the next demand. On the way, however, you might alienate those who would love to be your friends, and to learn from you.

When it comes to emotion you should do your best to explain the way you feel. Building up animosity for days, weeks or even months, doesn't really do anyone a lot of good, not even a Capricorn subject. People can't alter to suit your needs if they don't know what it is you want. For this reason you should always be as honest as you can be, even if this proves to be quite embarrassing at first. Be willing to show your flexible side – and even to create one if necessary. Try doing things the way others want to proceed now and again, despite the fact that you could be convinced that they are wrong in their approach. Allowing those around you the right to fail is important and in the end it will only make you look that much more confident and together when you stoop to pick up the pieces.

As often as proves to be possible you should display the inner smile that burns away inside you. Be willing to let your hair down and have a good time in the company of people who really do want to know that you are happy. Most important of all, share your inner honesty with those who are important to you.

The impressions you give

There is a great disparity between the way you feel about certain situations, and the impression you offer to an unsuspecting world. If you could fully see yourself as others usually see you, it's an odds-on certainty that you would be very surprised. The vast majority of those with whom you live and work see you as being ultra confident, very cool and quite capable. If you find this hard to believe, simply ask the most honest of your friends. It doesn't matter how you feel inside, or that you often have to dig around for answers that don't supply themselves immediately. What counts is the barrier that is placed constantly between your inner mind and your outward persona.

This is very important because it means you could get on in life even better than you may appear to be doing at the moment. Think what a great gift it is rarely to show that you are quaking inside. And when your cool approach means that you find advancement coming your way, you move on to the next set of requirements with the same apparent confidence you had before.

On a less positive note, it is possible that certain of the people with whom you interact on a daily basis could find you somewhat cold and even perhaps a little aloof on occasions. This is not the case, but once again there is a screen between the way you feel and the façade you show to the world at large. And though this barrier can be your best friend, it can also be a powerful enemy, especially in emotional or romantic situations. When circumstances necessitate, it is important that you tell those with whom you share your life exactly how you feel. That allows them to modify their own behaviour to suit your needs.

There may not be a great deal of work to do on altering your approach because in the main you are well liked and certainly respected. All that is really required in any case is an understanding that what you think and the way you act are not necessarily the same thing.

The way forward

Although it's true of course that anyone can make favourable alterations to their life, it's entirely possible that yours is already headed in the right direction generally. Capricorn people are not usually too complicated; they remain modest in their objectives and can achieve their ends through the medium of good ideas and hard work. You may not give the impression of being the most exciting person in the world – and nor do you wish to be. But when it's necessary to come up with the goods, mentally and practically, you don't usually have much trouble doing so.

To be and to remain quietly confident isn't too much to ask from life. Under most circumstances you take on tasks that you know you can achieve, try to be kind to others on the way and don't tend to make too many waves. It probably doesn't bother you too much that there are people around who may not care for you. This is essentially because you are a realist and understand that you won't be everyone's cup of tea.

If there are points within your nature that could be improved with effort they might relate to a certain stubborn streak. There are occasions when you become very determined to achieve a particular objective and you may not always listen to alternatives once you think you know how to proceed. However, since you don't tend to take on tasks that you are not equipped to deal with, what some may call intransigence, you might refer to as self-assurance. It is also possible that you sometimes find it difficult to express your inner feelings, and especially those related to love. You can be somewhat suspicious of the motives of others and may guard yourself a little too carefully as a result.

Try to recognise that there is more than one way to skin a cat, and that you can actually learn and grow through co-operation. You may also need to be willing to take on a greater degree of responsibility at work, even though this might go against the grain for a whole host of reasons. When faced with decisions that have a bearing on the lives of others, seek their counsel and take note of their opinions.

There are times when you can be a little too pessimistic for your own good. It is important to cultivate a cheerful approach, even though your sometimes slightly gloomy attitude is actually revered and smiled at by your friends. You are loyal, hard-working and generally kind. Capricorn may not be the most dynamic of the zodiac signs, but it is hard to fault it all the same.

CAPRICORN ON THE CUSP

Astrological profiles are altered for those people born at either the beginning or the end of a zodiac sign, or, more properly, on the cusps of a sign. In the case of Capricorn this would be on the 22nd of December and for two or three days after, and similarly at the end of the sign, probably from the 18th to the 20th of January.

The Sagittarius Cusp – 22nd to 24th December

Oh, what a lovely person you can be, and how respected you are by the world at large. At its best this is a very fortunate combination because it retains all the practical skills of Capricorn, but the nature is somewhat elevated by the quality of Sagittarius. Nothing much is beyond your capabilities but, unlike the typical Sagittarian, you back up your words with some quite practical actions. People learn to trust you and the amount of reliance that is placed on your judgement is sometimes staggering. Of course this does infer a high degree of responsibility but this fact probably won't worry you in the slightest. From a personal point of view you are very good to know and do your best to be friendly to almost everyone. However, you don't suffer fools at all gladly and probably prefer the company of those whose thoughts and ideas run along the same sort of road as yours.

Nobody could dispute the fact that you are very reasonable but you do sometimes get so obsessed with things that you could be less accessible than Sagittarius. A little extra work may be needed in this direction, especially when you are dealing with people who don't have your fast-track approach to problems. For all this you are a deep thinker and will often weigh up the pros and cons of a particular problem if necessary. In love you are deep and sincere, but with a superficial veneer that makes you appear light, bright and fun to be with. Making your way in life isn't at all difficult and money could easily come your way. This is not a response to good luck, but to dedication and inspired hard work.

With a good combination of the practical and the inspirational, you could turn your hand to almost anything. Your confidence is usually high and you are always in a good position to get by, no matter what obstacles you encounter. You like a challenge and rarely shy away from things when the going gets tough. This is one of the reasons that others like you so much and also explains why they have such confidence in your abilities. Your sense of purpose is strong and you may be tougher than you realise.

The Aquarius Cusp – 18th to 20th January

This is the more dreamy side of Capricorn and can make for an individual who is sometimes rather difficult for others to fathom. This is hardly surprising since you don't really know your own nature quite as well as you would wish. Because the two zodiac signs are a little like oil and water you can rub along quite nicely for ages as a typical Capricorn, before suddenly shooting off at a tangent into some nether world that isn't at all like the reliable sign of the Goat. You tend to think about things fairly deeply, though with a rather 'off the wall' approach that sometimes annoys your deeper Capricorn traits. Certainly you are fascinating to know, with a magnetic personality and a basic charm that shows itself a great deal, especially when your interest is roused.

You are a lover of mystery and might appear on occasion to have a slightly dark side. This is really only a sort of morbid curiosity and it doesn't reflect your own basic nature, which is kind, sincere and anxious to please. Socially you contribute to anything that takes your fancy but you won't stay around long if you find a conversation boring. Finding the right sort of romantic partner might be somewhat difficult because you are not run-of-the-mill and have strange needs at a personal level. However, once you have set your sights in a particular direction, you stick to it. And as far as finding the right person is concerned, you could do much worse than to trust your intuition, which is strong. You don't always know what you want from life, but this fact can prove to be half of the fascination.

This unusual nature tends to fit you for occupations that demand a variety of skills, though you may change your career entirely at some stage in your life. Certainly you can be very practical, but the way things feel is important to you and you might find that you start certain tasks time and again in order to make sure that they turn out just right. This sign combination can easily lead to a desire for travel and a need to extend your personal horizons. Your restlessness is sometimes a puzzle to others, but it's a fascination, too.

CAPRICORN AND ITS ASCENDANTS

The nature of every individual on the planet is composed of the rich variety of zodiac signs and planetary positions that were present at the time of their birth. Your Sun sign, which in your case is Capricorn, is one of the many factors when it comes to assessing the unique person you are. Probably the most important consideration, other than your Sun sign, is to establish the zodiac sign that was rising over the eastern horizon at the time that you were born. This is your Ascending or Rising sign. Most popular astrology fails to take account of the Ascendant, and yet its importance remains with you from the very moment of your birth, through every day of your life. The Ascendant is evident in the way you approach the world, and so, when meeting a person for the first time, it is this astrological influence that you are most likely to notice first. Our Ascending sign essentially represents what we appear to be, while the Sun sign is what we feel inside ourselves.

The Ascendant also has the potential for modifying our overall nature. For example, if you were born at a time of day when Capricorn was passing over the eastern horizon (this would be around the time of dawn) then you would be classed as a double Capricorn. As such, you would typify this zodiac sign, both internally and in your dealings with others. However, if your Ascendant sign turned out to be an Air sign, such as Gemini, there would be a profound alteration of nature, away from the expected qualities of Capricorn.

One of the reasons why popular astrology often ignores the Ascendant is that it has always been rather difficult to establish. We have found a way to make this possible by devising an easy-to-use table, which you will find on page 157 of this book. Using this, you can establish your Ascendant sign at a glance. You will need to know your rough time of birth, then it is simply a case of following the instructions.

For those readers who have no idea of their time of birth it might be worth allowing a good friend, or perhaps your partner, to read through the section that follows this introduction. Someone who deals with you on a regular basis may easily discover your Ascending sign, even though you could have some difficulty establishing it for yourself. A good understanding of this component of your nature is essential if you want to be aware of that 'other person' who is responsible for the way you make contact with the world at large. Your Sun sign, Ascendant sign, and the other pointers in this book will, together, allow you a far better understanding of what makes you tick as an individual. Peeling back the different layers of your astrological make-up can be an enlightening experience, and the Ascendant may represent one of the most important layers of all.

Capricorn with Capricorn Ascendant

Whatever it is that you are looking for in life, there isn't much doubt that you find it. Having done so, you tend to consolidate your position before looking ahead to the next set of objectives. There isn't a more determined soul than you in the length and breadth of the whole zodiac and you will not be thwarted once you have made up your mind. It would take an astute person to pull the wool over your eyes in any practical respect, though you may not be quite so clever when it comes to the personal side of your life. You can sometimes be rather misled in love, but not if you are as determined in this direction as you are in every other sphere of life.

The most enduring quality that you possess is staying-power, and you remain certain that your long-term plans are the right ones, modifying here and tweaking there to get them just right. On the way you make few deep friends, though the ones you do have tend to stay around for years. All the same you are popular, and can attract the right sort of people to help you out. In love you are sincere and honest, a good and reliable partner, and, I am told, one of the best lovers to be found in a month of Sundays. All you need to complete the picture is a more flexible attitude.

Capricorn with Aquarius Ascendant

Here the determination of Capricorn is assisted by a slightly more adaptable quality and an off-beat personality that tends to keep everyone else guessing. You don't care to be quite so predictable as the archetypal Capricorn would be and there is a more idealistic quality, or at least one that shows more. A greater number of friends than Capricorn would usually keep is likely, though less than a true Aquarian would gather. Few people doubt your sincerity, though not all of them understand what makes you tick. Unfortunately you are not in a position to help them out, because you are not very sure yourself. All the same you muddle through and can be very capable when the mood takes you.

Being a natural traveller, you love to see new places and would be quite fascinated by cultures that are very different to your own. People with this combination are inclined to spend some time living abroad and may even settle there. You look out for the underdog and will always have time for a good cause, no matter what it takes to help. In romantic terms you are a reliable partner, though with a slightly wayward edge which, if anything, tends to make you more attractive. Listen to your intuition, which rarely lets you down. Generally speaking you are very popular.

Capricorn with Pisces Ascendant

You are certainly not the easiest person in the world to understand, mainly because your nature is so deep and your personality so complicated, that others are somewhat intimidated at the prospect of staring into this abyss. All the same your friendly nature is attractive, and there will always be people around who are fascinated by the sheer magnetic quality that is endemic to the zodiac mix. Sentimental and extremely kind, there is no limit to the extent of your efforts on behalf of a deserving world, though there are some people around who wonder at your commitment and who may ridicule you a little for your staying-power, even in the face of some adversity. At work you are very capable, will work long and hard, and can definitely expect a greater degree of financial and practical success than Pisces alone. Routines don't bother you too much, though you do need regular periods of introspection, which help to recharge low batteries and a battered self-esteem.

In affairs of the heart you are somewhat given to impulse, which belies the more careful qualities of Capricorn. However, the determination remains intact and you are quite capable of chasing rainbows around, never realising that you can't get to the end of them. You are immensely lovable and a great favourite to many.

Capricorn with Aries Ascendant

If ever anyone could be accused of setting off immediately, but slowly, it has to be you. These are very contradictory signs and the differences will express themselves in a variety of ways. One thing is certain, you have tremendous tenacity and will see a job through patiently from beginning to end, without tiring on the way, and ensuring that every detail is taken care of properly. This combination often bestows good health and a great capacity for continuity, particularly in terms of the length of life. You are certainly not as argumentative as the typical Aries, but you do know how to get your own way, which is just as well because you are usually thinking on behalf of everyone else and not just on your own account.

At home you can relax, which is a blessing for Aries, though in fact you seldom choose to do so because you always have some project or other on the go. You probably enjoy knocking down and rebuilding walls, though this is a practical tendency and not responsive to relationships, in which you are ardent and sincere. Impetuosity is as close to your heart as is the case for any type of Aries subject, though you certainly have the ability to appear patient and steady. But it's really just a front, isn't it?

Capricorn with Taurus Ascendant

It might appear on the surface that you are not the most interesting person in the world. This is a pity, for you have an active though very logical mind, so logical in some instances that you would have a great deal in common with Mr Spock. This is the thorn in your flesh, or rather the flesh of everyone else, since you are probably quite happy being exactly what you are. You can think things through in a clear and very practical way and end up taking decisions that are balanced, eminently sensible, but, on occasions, rather dull.

Actually there is a fun machine somewhere deep within that Earth-sign nature and those who know you the best will recognise the fact. Often this combination is attended by a deep and biting sense of humour, but it's of the sort that less intelligent and considered types would find rather difficult to recognise. It is likely that you have no lack of confidence in your own judgement, and you have all the attributes necessary to do very well on the financial front. Slow and steady progress is your way and you need to be quite certain before you commit yourself to any new venture. This is a zodiac combination that can soak up years of stress and numerous difficulties and yet still come out on top. Nothing holds you back for long and you tend to be very brave.

Capricorn with Gemini Ascendant

A very careful and considered combination is evident here. You still have the friendly and chatty qualities of Gemini, though you also possess an astute, clever and deep-thinking quality which can really add bite to the Mercurial aspects of your nature. Although you rarely seem to take yourself or anyone else too seriously, in reality you are not easily fooled and usually know the direction in which you are heading. The practical application of your thought processes matter to you and you always give of your best, especially in any professional situation. This combination provides the very best business mind that any Gemini could have and, unlike other versions of the sign, you are willing to allow matters to mature. This quality cannot be overstated and leads to a form of ultimate achievement that many other Geminis would only guess at.

Family matters are important to you and your home is a special place of retreat, even though you are also willing to get out and meet the world, which is the prerogative of all Gemini types. There are times when you genuinely wish to remain quiet, and when such times arise you may need to explain the situation to some of the bemused people surrounding you. Above all you look towards material gain, though without ever losing your sense of humour.

Capricorn with Cancer Ascendant

The single most important factor here is the practical ability to get things done and to see any task, professional or personal, through to the end. Since half this combination is Cancer that also means expounding much of your energy on behalf of others. There isn't a charity in the world that would fail to recognise what a potent combination this is when it comes to the very concrete side of offering help and assistance. Many of your ideas hold water and you don't set off on abortive journeys of any kind, simply because you tend to get the ground rules fixed in your mind first.

On a more personal level you can be rather hard to get to know, because both these signs have a deep quality and a tendency to keep things in the dark. The mystery may only serve to encourage people to try and get to know you better. As a result you could attract a host of admirers, many of whom would wish to form romantic attachments. This may prove to be irrelevant however, because once you give your heart, you tend to be loyal and would only change your mind if you were pushed into doing so. Prolonged periods of inactivity don't do you any good and it is sensible for you to keep on the move, even though your progress in life is measured and very steady.

Capricorn with Leo Ascendant

What really sets you apart is your endless patience and your determination to get where you want to go, no matter how long it takes you to do so. On the way there are many sub-plots in your life and a wealth of entertaining situations to keep you amused. Probably somewhat quieter than the average Leo, you still have the capacity to be the life and soul of the party on those occasions when it suits you to be so. Energy, when allied to persistence, is a powerful commodity and you have a great need to take on causes of one sort or another. Probably at your best when defending the rights of the oppressed, you take the protecting qualities of Leo to greater heights than almost anyone else touched by the idealistic and regal qualities of the sign. If arguments come into your life, you deal with them quickly and, in the main, wisely. Like most Capricorn types you take to a few individuals, who will play a part in your life for years on end.

Being a good family type, your partner and children are very important and you will lavish the same patience, determination and ultimate success on their behalf that you do when dealing with more remote situations. The fact is that you do not know any other way to behave, and you are at your best when there is a mountain to climb.

Capricorn with Virgo Ascendant

Your endurance, persistence and concentration are legendary, and there is virtually nothing that eludes you once you have the bit between your teeth. You are not the pushy, fussy, go-getting sort of Virgoan but are steady, methodical and very careful. Once you have made up your mind, a whole team of wild horses could not change it, and although this can be a distinct blessing at times, it is a quality that can bring odd problems into your life too. The difficulty starts when you adopt a lost or less than sensible cause. Even in the face of overwhelming negative evidence, there is something inside you that prevents any sort of U-turn and so you carry on as solidly as only you can, to a destination that won't suit you at all.

There are few people around who are more loyal and constant than you can be. There is a lighter and brighter side to your nature, and the one or two people who are most important in your life will know how to bring it out. You have a wicked sense of humour, particularly if you have had a drink or when you are feeling on top form. Travel does you the world of good, even if there is a part of you that would rather stay at home. You have a potent, powerful and magnetic personality, but for much of the time it is kept carefully hidden.

Capricorn with Libra Ascendant

It is a fact that Libra is the most patient of the Air signs, though like the others it needs to get things done fairly quickly. Capricorn, on the other hand, will work long and hard to achieve its objectives and will not be thwarted. As a result this is a powerful combination and one that leads ultimately to success.

Capricorn is often accused of taking itself too seriously, and yet it has an ironic and really very funny sense of humour which only its chief confidants recognise. Libra is lighthearted, always willing to have fun and quite anxious to please. When these two basic types come together in their best forms, you might find yourself to be one of the most well- balanced people around. Certainly you know what you want, but don't have to use a bulldozer in order to get it.

Active and enthusiastic when something really takes your fancy, you might also turn out to be one of the very best lovers of them all. The reason for this is that you have the depth of Capricorn but the lighter and more directly affectionate qualities of the Scales. What you want from life in a personal sense, you eventually tend to get, but you don't care too much if this takes you a while. Few people could deny that you are a faithful friend, a happy sort and a deeply magnetic personality.

Capricorn with Scorpio Ascendant

If patience, perseverance and a solid ability to get where you want to go are considered to be the chief components of a happy life, then you should be skipping about every day. Unfortunately this is not always the case, and here we have two zodiac signs who can both be too deep for their own good. Both Scorpio and Capricorn are inclined to take themselves rather too seriously, and your main lesson in life, and some would say the reason you have adopted this zodiac combination, is to 'lighten up'. If all that determination is pushed in the direction of your service to the world at large, you are seen as being one of the kindest people imaginable. This is really the only option for you, because if you turn this tremendous potential power inwards all the time you will become brooding, secretive and sometimes even selfish. Your eyes should be turned towards a needy humanity, which can be served with the dry but definite wit of Capricorn and the true compassion of Scorpio.

It is impossible with this combination to indicate what areas of life suit you the best. Certainly you adore luxury in all its forms, and yet you can get by with almost nothing. You desire travel, and at the same time love the comforts and stability of home. The people who know you best are aware that you are rather special. Listen to what they say.

Capricorn with Sagittarius Ascendant

The typical Sagittarian nature is modified for the better when Capricorn is part of the deal. It's true that you manage to push forward progressively under most circumstances, but you also possess staying power and can work long and hard to achieve your objectives, most of which are carefully planned in advance. Few people have the true measure of your nature, for it runs rather deeper than appears to be the case on the surface. Routines don't bother you as much as would be the case for Sagittarius when taken alone, and you don't care if any objective takes weeks, months or even years to achieve. You are very fond of those you take to and would certainly prove to be a capable friend, even when things get quite tough.

In love relationships you are steadfast and reliable, and yet you never lose the ability to entertain. Yours is a dry sense of humour which shows itself to a multitude of different people and which doesn't run out, even on those occasions when life gets tough. It might take you a long time to find the love of your life, but when you do there is a greater possibility of retaining the relationship for a long period. You don't tend to inherit money, but you can easily make it for yourself, though you won't worry too much about the amount. On the whole you are a very self-sufficient and sensible individual.

THE MOON AND THE PART IT PLAYS IN YOUR LIFE

In astrology the Moon is probably the single most important heavenly body after the Sun. Its unique position, as partner to the Earth on its journey around the solar system, means that the Moon appears to pass through the signs of the zodiac extremely quickly. The zodiac position of the Moon at the time of your birth plays a great part in personal character and is especially significant in the build-up of your emotional nature.

Your Own Moon Sign

Discovering the position of the Moon at the time of your birth has always been notoriously difficult because tracking the complex zodiac positions of the Moon is not easy. This process has been reduced to three simple stages with our Lunar Tables. A breakdown of the Moon's zodiac positions can be found from page 35 onwards, so that once you know what your Moon Sign is, you can see what part this plays in the overall build-up of your personal character.

If you follow the instructions on the next page you will soon be able to work out exactly what zodiac sign the Moon occupied on the day that you were born and you can then go on to compare the reading for this position with those of your Sun sign and your Ascendant. It is partly the comparison between these three important positions that goes towards making you the unique individual you are.

HOW TO DISCOVER YOUR MOON SIGN

This is a three-stage process. You may need a pen and a piece of paper but if you follow the instructions below the process should only take a minute or so.

STAGE 1 First of all you need to know the Moon Age at the time of your birth. If you look at Moon Table 1, on page 33, you will find all the years between 1919 and 2017 down the left side. Find the year of your birth and then trace across to the right to the month of your birth. Where the two intersect you will find a number. This is the date of the New Moon in the month that you were born. You now need to count forward the number of days between the New Moon and your own birthday. For example, if the New Moon in the month of your birth was shown as being the 6th and you were born on the 20th, your Moon Age Day would be 14. If the New Moon in the month of your birth came after your birthday, you need to count forward from the New Moon in the previous month, which, if you were born in January, means you must look at December in the previous year. You cannot count from December in the year of your birth, as that month is *after* your birth. Whatever the result, jot this number down so that you do not forget it.

STAGE 2 Take a look at Moon Table 2 on page 34. Down the left hand column look for the date of your birth. Now trace across to the month of your birth. Where the two meet you will find a letter. Copy this letter down alongside your Moon Age Day.

STAGE 3 Moon Table 3 on page 34 will supply you with the zodiac sign the Moon occupied on the day of your birth. Look for your Moon Age Day down the left hand column and then for the letter you found in Stage 2. Where the two converge you will find a zodiac sign and this is the sign occupied by the Moon on the day that you were born.

Your Zodiac Moon Sign Explained

You will find a profile of all zodiac Moon Signs on pages 35 to 38, showing in yet another way how astrology helps to make you into the individual that you are. In each daily entry of the Astral Diary you can find the zodiac position of the Moon for every day of the year. This also allows you to discover your lunar birthdays. Since the Moon passes through all the signs of the zodiac in about a month, you can expect something like twelve lunar birthdays each year. At these times you are likely to be emotionally steady and able to make the sort of decisions that have real, lasting value.

MOON TABLE 1

YEAR	NOV	DEC	JAN	YEAR	NOV	DEC	JAN	YEAR	NOV	DEC	JAN
1919	22	21	1/31	1952	17	17	26	1985	12	12	21
1920	10	10	20	1953	6	6	15	1986	2	1/30	10
1921	29	29	9	1954	25	25	5	1987	21	20	29
1922	19	18	27	1955	14	14	24	1988	9	9	19
1923	8	8	17	1956	2	2	13	1989	28	28	7
1924	26	26	6	1957	21	21	1/30	1990	17	17	26
1925	16	15	24	1958	11	10	19	1991	6	6	15
1926	5	5	14	1959	30	29	9	1992	24	24	4
1927	24	24	3	1960	19	18	27	1993	14	14	22
1928	12	12	21	1961	8	7	16	1994	3	2	11
1929	1	1/30	11	1962	27	26	6	1995	22	22	1
1930	20	19	29	1963	15	15	25	1996	11	10	20
1931	9	9	18	1964	4	4	14	1997	30	29	9
1932	27	27	7	1965	22	22	3	1998	19	18	28
1933	17	17	25	1966	12	12	21	1999	8	7	17
1934	7	6	15	1967	2	1/30	10	2000	27	25	6
1935	26	25	5	1968	21	20	29	2001	16	15	24
1936	14	13	24	1969	9	9	19	2002	4	4	13
1937	3	2	12	1970	29	28	7	2003	24	23	3
1938	22	21	1/31	1971	18	17	26	2004	11	11	21
1939	11	10	20	1972	6	6	15	2005	1	1	10
1940	29	28	9	1973	25	25	5	2006	20	20	29
1941	19	18	27	1974	14	14	24	2007	9	9	18
1942	8	8	16	1975	3	3	12	2008	28	27	8
1943	27	27	6	1976	21	21	1/31	2009	17	16	26
1944	15	15	25	1977	11	10	19	2010	6	6	15
1945	4	4	14	1978	30	29	9	2011	25	25	4
1946	23	23	3	1979	19	18	27	2012	13	12	23
1947	12	12	21	1980	8	7	16	2013	2	2	12
1948	1	1/30	11	1981	26	26	6	2014	22	22	1/31
1949	20	19	29	1982	15	15	25	2015	11	20	19
1950	9	9	18	1983	4	4	14	2016	29	29	9
1951	29	28	7	1984	22	22	3	2017	18	18	27

TABLE 2

DAY	DEC	JAN
1	i	A
2	i	A
3	m	A
4	m	A
5	n	A
6	n	A
7	n	A
8	n	A
9	n	A
10	n	A
11	n	B
12	n	B
13	n	B
14	n	B
15	n	B
16	n	B
17	n	B
18	n	B
19	n	B
20	n	B
21	n	C
22	n	C
23	q	C
24	q	C
25	q	C
26	q	C
27	q	C
28	q	C
29	q	C
30	q	C
31	q	C

MOON TABLE 3

M/D	i	m	n	q	A	B	C
0	SA	SA	SA	CP	CP	AQ	AQ
1	SA	SA	CP	CP	AQ	AQ	AQ
2	CP	CP	CP	AQ	AQ	AQ	PI
3	CP	CP	AQ	AQ	AQ	PI	PI
4	CP	AQ	AQ	PI	PI	PI	AR
5	AQ	AQ	PI	PI	PI	AR	AR
6	AQ	AQ	PI	AR	AR	AR	AR
7	PI	PI	AR	AR	AR	AR	TA
8	PI	PI	AR	AR	AR	TA	TA
9	AR	AR	TA	TA	TA	TA	GE
10	AR	AR	TA	TA	TA	GE	GE
11	TA	TA	TA	GE	GE	GE	GE
12	TA	TA	GE	GE	GE	GE	CA
13	GE	GE	GE	GE	GE	CA	CA
14	GE	GE	CA	CA	CA	CA	LE
15	GE	GE	GE	CA	CA	LE	LE
16	GE	CA	CA	CA	LE	LE	LE
17	CA	CA	CA	LE	LE	LE	VI
18	CA	CA	LE	LE	LE	VI	VI
19	CA	LE	LE	LE	VI	VI	VI
20	LE	LE	LE	VI	VI	LI	LI
21	LE	LE	VI	VI	LI	LI	LI
22	VI	VI	VI	LI	LI	LI	SC
23	VI	VI	VI	LI	LI	SC	SC
24	VI	VI	LI	LI	SC	SC	SC
25	LI	LI	LI	SC	SC	SA	SA
26	LI	LI	SC	SC	SA	SA	SA
27	SC	SC	SC	SA	SA	SA	CP
28	SC	SC	SC	SA	SA	CP	CP
29	SC	SA	SA	SA	CP	CP	CP

AR = Aries, TA = Taurus, GE = Gemini, CA = Cancer, LE = Leo, VI = Virgo, LI = Libra, SC = Scorpio, SA = Sagittarius, CP = Capricorn, AQ = Aquarius, PI = Pisces

MOON SIGNS

Moon in Aries

You have a strong imagination, courage, determination and a desire to do things in your own way and forge your own path through life.

Originality is a key attribute; you are seldom stuck for ideas although your mind is changeable and you could take the time to focus on individual tasks. Often quick-tempered, you take orders from few people and live life at a fast pace. Avoid health problems by taking regular time out for rest and relaxation.

Emotionally, it is important that you talk to those you are closest to and work out your true feelings. Once you discover that people are there to help, there is less necessity for you to do everything yourself.

Moon in Taurus

The Moon in Taurus gives you a courteous and friendly manner, which means you are likely to have many friends.

The good things in life mean a lot to you, as Taurus is an Earth sign that delights in experiences which please the senses. Hence you are probably a lover of good food and drink, which may in turn mean you need to keep an eye on the bathroom scales, especially as looking good is also important to you.

Emotionally you are fairly stable and you stick by your own standards. Taureans do not respond well to change. Intuition also plays an important part in your life.

Moon in Gemini

You have a warm-hearted character, sympathetic and eager to help others. At times reserved, you can also be articulate and chatty: this is part of the paradox of Gemini, which always brings duplicity to the nature. You are interested in current affairs, have a good intellect, and are good company and likely to have many friends. Most of your friends have a high opinion of you and would be ready to defend you should the need arise. However, this is usually unnecessary, as you are quite capable of defending yourself in any verbal confrontation.

Travel is important to your inquisitive mind and you find intellectual stimulus in mixing with people from different cultures. You also gain much from reading, writing and the arts but you do need plenty of rest and relaxation in order to avoid fatigue.

Moon in Cancer

The Moon in Cancer at the time of birth is a fortunate position as Cancer is the Moon's natural home. This means that the qualities of compassion and understanding given by the Moon are especially enhanced in your nature, and you are friendly and sociable and cope well with emotional pressures. You cherish home and family life, and happily do the domestic tasks. Your surroundings are important to you and you hate squalor and filth. You are likely to have a love of music and poetry.

Your basic character, although at times changeable like the Moon itself, depends on symmetry. You aim to make your surroundings comfortable and harmonious, for yourself and those close to you.

Moon in Leo

The best qualities of the Moon and Leo come together to make you warm-hearted, fair, ambitious and self-confident. With good organisational abilities, you invariably rise to a position of responsibility in your chosen career. This is fortunate as you don't enjoy being an 'also-ran' and would rather be an important part of a small organisation than a menial in a large one.

You should be lucky in love, and happy, provided you put in the effort to make a comfortable home for yourself and those close to you. It is likely that you will have a love of pleasure, sport, music and literature. Life brings you many rewards, most of them as a direct result of your own efforts, although you may be luckier than average and ready to make the best of any situation.

Moon in Virgo

You are endowed with good mental abilities and a keen receptive memory, but you are never ostentatious or pretentious. Naturally quite reserved, you still have many friends, especially of the opposite sex. Marital relationships must be discussed carefully and worked at so that they remain harmonious, as personal attachments can be a problem if you do not give them your full attention.

Talented and persevering, you possess artistic qualities and are a good homemaker. Earning your honours through genuine merit, you work long and hard towards your objectives but show little pride in your achievements. Many short journeys will be undertaken in your life.

Moon in Libra

With the Moon in Libra you are naturally popular and make friends easily. People like you, probably more than you realise, you bring fun to a party and are a natural diplomat. For all its good points, Libra is not the most stable of astrological signs and, as a result, your emotions can be a little unstable too. Therefore, although the Moon in Libra is said to be good for love and marriage, your Sun sign and Rising sign will have an important effect on your emotional and loving qualities.

You must remember to relate to others in your decision-making. Co-operation is crucial because Libra represents the 'balance' of life that can only be achieved through harmonious relationships. Conformity is not easy for you because Libra, an Air sign, likes its independence.

Moon in Scorpio

Some people might call you pushy. In fact, all you really want to do is to live life to the full and protect yourself and your family from the pressures of life. Take care to avoid giving the impression of being sarcastic or impulsive and use your energies wisely and constructively.

You have great courage and you invariably achieve your goals by force of personality and sheer effort. You are fond of mystery and are good at predicting the outcome of situations and events. Travel experiences can be beneficial to you.

You may experience problems if you do not take time to examine your motives in a relationship, and also if you allow jealousy, always a feature of Scorpio, to cloud your judgement.

Moon in Sagittarius

The Moon in Sagittarius helps to make you a generous individual with humanitarian qualities and a kind heart. Restlessness may be intrinsic as your mind is seldom still. Perhaps because of this, you have a need for change that could lead you to several major moves during your adult life. You are not afraid to stand your ground when you know your judgement is right, you speak directly and have good intuition.

At work you are quick, efficient and versatile and so you make an ideal employee. You need work to be intellectually demanding and do not enjoy tedious routines.

In relationships, you anger quickly if faced with stupidity or deception, though you are just as quick to forgive and forget. Emotionally, there are times when your heart rules your head.

Moon in Capricorn

The Moon in Capricorn makes you popular and likely to come into the public eye in some way. The watery Moon is not entirely comfortable in the Earth sign of Capricorn and this may lead to some difficulties in the early years of life. An initial lack of creative ability and indecision must be overcome before the true qualities of patience and perseverance inherent in Capricorn can show through.

You have good administrative ability and are a capable worker, and if you are careful you can accumulate wealth. But you must be cautious and take professional advice in partnerships, as you are open to deception. You may be interested in social or welfare work, which suit your organisational skills and sympathy for others.

Moon in Aquarius

The Moon in Aquarius makes you an active and agreeable person with a friendly, easy-going nature. Sympathetic to the needs of others, you flourish in a laid-back atmosphere. You are broad-minded, fair and open to suggestion, although sometimes you have an unconventional quality which others can find hard to understand.

You are interested in the strange and curious, and in old articles and places. You enjoy trips to these places and gain much from them. Political, scientific and educational work interests you and you might choose a career in science or technology.

Money-wise, you make gains through innovation and concentration and Lunar Aquarians often tackle more than one job at a time. In love you are kind and honest.

Moon in Pisces

You have a kind, sympathetic nature, somewhat retiring at times, but you always take account of others' feelings and help when you can.

Personal relationships may be problematic, but as life goes on you can learn from your experiences and develop a better understanding of yourself and the world around you.

You have a fondness for travel, appreciate beauty and harmony and hate disorder and strife. You may be fond of literature and would make a good writer or speaker yourself. You have a creative imagination and may come across as an incurable romantic. You have strong intuition, maybe bordering on a mediumistic quality, which sets you apart from the mass. You may not be rich in cash terms, but your personal gifts are worth more than gold.

CAPRICORN IN LOVE

Discover how compatible in love you are with people from the same and other signs of the zodiac. Five stars equals a match made in heaven!

Capricorn meets Capricorn

One of the best combinations because Capricorn knows what it wants and likes its partner to be the same. This may not be the deepest or most passionate of relationships, but Capricorn is adaptable enough to accept that. Material success is likely for this couple as they share the ability to move slowly towards even distant horizons. There will be words of love and a generally happy family atmosphere, and although at times the relationship may look lukewarm, it will usually remain strong and secure. Star rating: *****

Capricorn meets Aquarius

Probably one of the least likely combinations as Capricorn and Aquarius are unlikely to choose each other in the first place, unless one side is quite untypical of their sign. Capricorn approaches things in a practical way and likes to get things done, while Aquarius works almost exclusively for the moment and relies heavily on intuition. Their attitudes to romance are also diametrically opposed: Aquarius' moods tend to swing from red hot to ice cold in a minute, which is alien to steady Capricorn. Star rating: **

Capricorn meets Pisces

There is some chance of a happy relationship here, but it will need work on both sides. Capricorn is a go-getter, but likes to plan long term. Pisces is naturally more immediate, but has enough intuition to understand the Goat's thinking. Both have patience, but it will usually be Pisces who chooses to play second fiddle. The quiet nature of both signs might be a problem, as someone will have to lead, especially in social situations. Both signs should recognise this fact and accommodate it. Star rating: ***

Capricorn meets Aries

Capricorn works conscientiously to achieve its objectives and so can be the perfect companion for Aries. The Ram knows how to achieve but not how to consolidate, so the two signs have a great deal to offer one another practically. There may not be fireworks and it's sometimes doubtful how well they know each other, but it may not matter. Aries is outwardly hot but inwardly cool, whilst Capricorn can appear low-key but be a furnace underneath. Such a pairing can gradually find contentment, though both parties may wonder how this is so. Star rating: ****

Capricorn meets Taurus

If not quite a match made in heaven, this comes close. Both signs are Earthy in nature and that is a promising start. Capricorn is very practical and can make a Taurean's dreams come true. Both are tidy, like to know what is going to happen in a day-to-day sense, and are steady and committed. Taurus loves refinement, which Capricorn accepts and even helps to create. A good prognosis for material success rounds off a relationship that could easily stay the course. The only thing missing is a genuine sense of humour. Star rating: *****

Capricorn meets Gemini

Gemini has a natural fondness for Capricorn, which at first may be mutual. However, Capricorn is very organised, practical and persevering, and always achieves its goals in the end. Gemini starts out like this, but then starts to use a more instinctive and evolutionary approach, which may interfere with mutual objectives. To compensate, Gemini helps Capricorn avoid taking itself too seriously, while Capricorn brings a degree of stability into Gemini's world. When this pairing does work, though, it will be spectacular! Star rating: ***

Capricorn meets Cancer

Just about the only thing this pair have in common is the fact that both signs begin 'Ca'! Some signs of the zodiac are instigators and some are reactors, and both the Crab and the Goat are reactors. Consequently, they both need incentives from their partners but won't find it in each other and, with neither side taking the initiative, there's a spark missing. Cancer and Capricorn do think alike in some ways and so, if they can find their common purpose, they can be as happy as anyone. It's just rather unlikely. Star rating: **

Capricorn meets Leo

Despite promising appearances, this match often fails to take. Capricorn focuses on long-term objectives and, like Leo, is very practical. Both signs are capable of attaining success after a struggle, which, while requiring effort, gives them a mutual goal. But when life is easier, the cracks begin to show. Capricorn can be too serious for Leo, and the couple share few ideals. Leo loves luxury, Capricorn seeks austerity. Leo is warm but Capricorn seems cold and wintry in comparison. Both have many good points, but they don't seem to fire each other off properly. Star rating: **

Capricorn meets Virgo

One of the best possible combinations, because Virgo and Capricorn have an instinctive understanding. Both signs know the value of dedicated hard work and apply it equally in a relationship and other areas of life. Two of the most practical signs, nothing is beyond their ken, even if to outsiders they appear rather sterile or lacking in 'oomph'. What matters most is that the individuals are happy and with so much in common, the likelihood of mutual material success, and a shared devotion to home and family, there isn't much doubt of that. Star rating: *****

Capricorn meets Libra

Libra and Capricorn rub each other up the wrong way because their attitudes to life are so different, and although both are capable of doing something about this, in reality they probably won't. Capricorn is steady, determined and solid, while Libra is bright but sometimes superficial and not entirely reliable. They usually lack the instant spark needed to get them together in the first place, so when it does happen it is often because one of the partners is not very typical of their sign. Star rating: **

Capricorn meets Scorpio

Lack of communication is the governing factor here. Neither of this pair are renowned communicators and both need a partner to draw out their full verbal potential. Consequently, Scorpio may find Capricorn cold and unapproachable while Capricorn could find Scorpio dark and brooding. Both are naturally tidy and would keep a pristine house but great effort and a mutual goal is needed on both sides to overcome the missing spark. A good match on the financial side, but probably not an earth shattering personal encounter. Star rating: **

Capricorn meets Sagittarius

Any real problem here will stem from a lack of understanding. Capricorn is very practical and needs to be constantly on the go – though in a fairly low-key sort of way. Sagittarius is busy too, though always in a panic and invariably behind its deadlines, which will annoy organised Capricorn. Sagittarius doesn't really have the depth of nature that best suits an Earth sign like Capricorn and its flirty nature could upset the sensitive Goat, but their lighter attitude could be cheering, too. Star rating: ***

VENUS: THE PLANET OF LOVE

If you look up at the sky around sunset or sunrise you will often see Venus in close attendance to the Sun. It is arguably one of the most beautiful sights of all and there is little wonder that historically it became associated with the goddess of love. But although Venus is important in your attitude to love and in the way others see you romantically, this is only one of its spheres of influence.

Venus plays a part in the cultured side of your life and has much to do with your appreciation of art, literature, music and general creativity. Even the way you look is responsive to the part of the zodiac that Venus occupied at the start of your life, though this is also down to your Sun sign and Ascending sign. If, at the time you were born, Venus occupied one of the more gregarious zodiac signs, you will be open in love, as well as more attracted to entertainment, social gatherings and good company. If on the other hand Venus occupied a quiet zodiac sign at the time of your birth, you would tend to be more retiring and less willing to shine in public situations.

Venus can have a great bearing on your outward appearance and since we all have to mix with others, knowledge of Venus' position at your birth can help you learn to make the best of what it has to offer you.

One of the great complications in the past has always been trying to establish exactly what zodiac position Venus enjoyed when you were born because the planet is notoriously difficult to track. Here we have created an exclusive table for your Sun sign, shown on the next page.

To calculate your Venus sign, first look up the year of your birth in the table. As Capricorn naturally spans two calendar years every time it comes around, double-check that you are looking at the right line. The table is organised so that December is always the first month, so, for instance, if you were born in December 1940 or January 1941 you would look at the column for 1940–1, because the year on the calendar has changed while the zodiac is still in the sign of Capricorn. If you were born in January 1942 you would look at the column for 1941–2. Once you have the right column, you will see a sign of the zodiac next to the date. This was the sign that Venus occupied in that year. If Venus occupied more than one sign during the period, this is indicated by the date on which the sign changed and the name of the new sign. For instance, if you are looking at the years 1940–1, Venus was in Sagittarius until the 15th January, after which time it was in Capricorn. If you were born before 15th January your Venus sign is Sagittarius, if you were born on or after 15th January, your Venus sign is Capricorn. Once you have established the position of Venus at the time of your birth, you can then look in the pages which follow to see how this has a bearing on your life.

1919–20 SCORPIO/5.1 SAGITTARIUS
1920–1 AQUARIUS/7.1 PISCES
1921–2 SAGITTARIUS/30.12 CAPRICORN
1922–3 SCORPIO/6.1 SAGITTARIUS
1923–4 CAPRICORN/
26.12 AQUARIUS/19.1 PISCES
1924–5 SAGITTARIUS/15.1 CAPRICORN
1925–6 AQUARIUS
1926–7 CAPRICORN/9.1 AQUARIUS
1927–8 SCORPIO/4.1 SAGITTARIUS
1928–9 AQUARIUS/6.1 PISCES
1929–30 SAGITTARIUS/29.12
CAPRICORN
1930–1 SCORPIO/3.1 SAGITTARIUS
1931–2 CAPRICORN/
26.12 AQUARIUS/19.1 PISCES
1932–3 SAGITTARIUS/15.1 PISCES
1933–4 AQUARIUS
1934–5 CAPRICORN/9.1 AQUARIUS
1935–6 SCORPIO/4.1 SAGITTARIUS
1936–7 AQUARIUS/6.1 PISCES
1937–8 SAGITTARIUS/29.12 CAPRICORN
1938–9 SCORPIO/3.1 SAGITTARIUS
1939–40 CAPRICORN/
25.12 AQUARIUS/18.1 PISCES
1940–1 SAGITTARIUS/15.1 CAPRICORN
1941–2 AQUARIUS
1942–3 CAPRICORN/8.1 AQUARIUS
1943–4 SCORPIO/3.1 SAGITTARIUS
1944–5 AQUARIUS/5.1 PISCES
1945–6 SAGITTARIUS/28.12 CAPRICORN
1946–7 SCORPIO/3.1 SAGITTARIUS
1947–8 CAPRICORN/
25.12 AQUARIUS/18.1 PISCES
1948–9 SAGITTARIUS/14.1 CAPRICORN
1949–50 AQUARIUS
1950–1 CAPRICORN/8.1 AQUARIUS
1951–2 SCORPIO/3.1 SAGITTARIUS
1952–3 AQUARIUS/5.1 PISCES
1953–4 SAGITTARIUS/28.12 CAPRICORN
1954–5 SCORPIO/4.1 SAGITTARIUS
1955–6 CAPRICORN/
24.12 AQUARIUS/17.1 PISCES
1956–7 SAGITTARIUS/14.1 CAPRICORN
1957–8 AQUARIUS
1958–9 CAPRICORN/7.1 AQUARIUS
1959–60 SCORPIO/2.1 SAGITTARIUS
1960–1 AQUARIUS/5.1 PISCES
1961–2 SAGITTARIUS/28.12 CAPRICORN
1962–3 SCORPIO/4.1 SAGITTARIUS
1963–4 CAPRICORN/
24.12 AQUARIUS/17.1 PISCES
1964–5 SAGITTARIUS/13.1 CAPRICORN
1965–6 AQUARIUS
1966–7 CAPRICORN/7.1 AQUARIUS
1967–8 SCORPIO/2.1 SAGITTARIUS
1968–9 AQUARIUS/5.1 PISCES
1969–70 SAGITTARIUS/
27.12 CAPRICORN
1970–1 SCORPIO/5.1 SAGITTARIUS
1971–2 CAPRICORN/
23.12 AQUARIUS/16.1 PISCES
1972–3 SAGITTARIUS/12.1 CAPRICORN
1973–4 AQUARIUS
1974–5 CAPRICORN/6.1 AQUARIUS
1975–6 SCORPIO/1.1 SAGITTARIUS
1976–7 AQUARIUS/4.1 PISCES
1977–8 SAGITTARIUS/27.12 CAPRICORN
1978–9 SCORPIO/5.1 SAGITTARIUS
1979–80 CAPRICORN/
23.12 AQUARIUS/16.1 PISCES
1980–1 SAGITTARIUS/12.1 CAPRICORN
1981–2 AQUARIUS
1982–3 CAPRICORN/6.1 AQUARIUS
1983–4 SCORPIO/1.1 SAGITTARIUS
1984–5 AQUARIUS/4.1 PISCES
1985–6 SAGITTARIUS/27.12 CAPRICORN
1986–7 SCORPIO/6.1 SAGITTARIUS
1987–8 AQUARIUS/15.1 PISCES
1988–9 SAGITTARIUS/11.1 CAPRICORN
1989–90 AQUARIUS/17.1 CAPRICORN
1990–1 CAPRICORN/5.1 AQUARIUS
1991–2 SCORPIO/1.1 SAGITTARIUS
1992–3 AQUARIUS/4.1 PISCES
1993–4 SAGITTARIUS/26.12 CAPRICORN
1994–5 SCORPIO/7.1 SAGITTARIUS
1995–6 AQUARIUS/15.1 PISCES
1996–7 SAGITTARIUS/11.1 CAPRICORN
1997–8 AQUARIUS/14.1 CAPRICORN
1998–9 CAPRICORN/5.1 AQUARIUS
1999–2000 SCORPIO/1.1 SAGITTARIUS
2000–01 SAGITTARIUS/
26.12 CAPRICORN
2001–02 CAPRICORN/4.1 AQUARIUS
2002–03 SAGITTARIUS/
26.12 CAPRICORN
2003–04 SCORPIO/7.1 SAGITTARIUS
2004–05 SAGITTARIUS/
30.12 CAPRICORN
2005–06 AQUARIUS / 2.1 CAPRICORN
2006–07 AQUARIUS/14.1 CAPRICORN
2007–08 CAPRICORN / 5.1 AQUARIUS
2008–09 SCORPIO / 1.1 SAGITTARIUS
2009–10 SAGITTARIUS /
26.12 CAPRICORN
2010–11 SAGITTARIUS/
26.12 CAPRICORN
2011–12 CAPRICORN / 4.12 AQUARIUS
2012–13 AQUARIUS/14.1 CAPRICORN
2013–14 CAPRICORN / 5.1 AQUARIUS
2014–15 AQUARIUS/14.1 CAPRICORN
2015–16 CAPRICORN / 5.1 AQUARIUS
2016–17 AQUARIUS / 1.1 SAGITTARIUS
2017 SAGITTARIUS / 26.12 CAPRICORN

VENUS THROUGH THE ZODIAC SIGNS

Venus in Aries

Amongst other things, the position of Venus in Aries indicates a fondness for travel, music and all creative pursuits. Your nature tends to be affectionate and you would try not to create confusion or difficulty for others if it could be avoided. Many people with this planetary position have a great love of the theatre, and mental stimulation is of the greatest importance. Early romantic attachments are common with Venus in Aries, so it is very important to establish a genuine sense of romantic continuity. Early marriage is not recommended, especially if it is based on sympathy. You may give your heart a little too readily on occasions.

Venus in Taurus

You are capable of very deep feelings and your emotions tend to last for a very long time. This makes you a trusting partner and lover, whose constancy is second to none. In life you are precise and careful and always try to do things the right way. Although this means an ordered life, which you are comfortable with, it can also lead you to be rather too fussy for your own good. Despite your pleasant nature, you are very fixed in your opinions and quite able to speak your mind. Others are attracted to you and historical astrologers always quoted this position of Venus as being very fortunate in terms of marriage. However, if you find yourself involved in a failed relationship, it could take you a long time to trust again.

Venus in Gemini

As with all associations related to Gemini, you tend to be quite versatile, anxious for change and intelligent in your dealings with the world at large. You may gain money from more than one source but you are equally good at spending it. There is an inference here that you are a good communicator, via either the written or the spoken word, and you love to be in the company of interesting people. Always on the look-out for culture, you may also be very fond of music, and love to indulge the curious and cultured side of your nature. In romance you tend to have more than one relationship and could find yourself associated with someone who has previously been a friend or even a distant relative.

Venus in Cancer

You often stay close to home because you are very fond of family and enjoy many of your most treasured moments when you are with those you love. Being naturally sympathetic, you will always do anything you can to support those around you, even people you hardly know at all. This charitable side of your nature is your most noticeable trait and is one of the reasons why others are naturally so fond of you. Being receptive and in some cases even psychic, you can see through to the soul of most of those with whom you come into contact. You may not commence too many romantic attachments but when you do give your heart, it tends to be unconditionally.

Venus in Leo

It must become quickly obvious to almost anyone you meet that you are kind, sympathetic and yet determined enough to stand up for anyone or anything that is truly important to you. Bright and sunny, you warm the world with your natural enthusiasm and would rarely do anything to hurt those around you, or at least not intentionally. In romance you are ardent and sincere, though some may find your style just a little overpowering. Gains come through your contacts with other people and this could be especially true with regard to romance, for love and money often come hand in hand for those who were born with Venus in Leo. People claim to understand you, though you are more complex than you seem.

Venus in Virgo

Your nature could well be fairly quiet no matter what your Sun sign might be, though this fact often manifests itself as an inner peace and would not prevent you from being basically sociable. Some delays and even the odd disappointment in love cannot be ruled out with this planetary position, though it's a fact that you will usually find the happiness you look for in the end. Catapulting yourself into romantic entanglements that you know to be rather ill-advised is not sensible, and it would be better to wait before you committed yourself exclusively to any one person. It is the essence of your nature to serve the world at large and through doing so it is possible that you will attract money at some stage in your life.

Venus in Libra

Venus is very comfortable in Libra and bestows upon those people who have this planetary position a particular sort of kindness that is easy to recognise. This is a very good position for all sorts of friendships and also for romantic attachments that usually bring much joy into your life. Few individuals with Venus in Libra would avoid marriage and since you are capable of great depths of love, it is likely that you will find a contented personal life. You like to mix with people of integrity and intelligence but don't take kindly to scruffy surroundings or work that means getting your hands too dirty. Careful speculation, good business dealings and money through marriage all seem fairly likely.

Venus in Scorpio

You are quite open and tend to spend money quite freely, even on those occasions when you don't have very much. Although your intentions are always good, there are times when you get yourself in to the odd scrape and this can be particularly true when it comes to romance, which you may come to late or from a rather unexpected direction. Certainly you have the power to be happy and to make others contented on the way, but you find the odd stumbling block on your journey through life and it could seem that you have to work harder than those around you. As a result of this, you gain a much deeper understanding of the true value of personal happiness than many people ever do, and are likely to achieve true contentment in the end.

Venus in Sagittarius

You are lighthearted, cheerful and always able to see the funny side of any situation. These facts enhance your popularity, which is especially high with members of the opposite sex. You should never have to look too far to find romantic interest in your life, though it is just possible that you might be too willing to commit yourself before you are certain that the person in question is right for you. Part of the problem here extends to other areas of life too. The fact is that you like variety in everything and so can tire of situations that fail to offer it. All the same, if you choose wisely and learn to understand your restless side, then great happiness can be yours.

Venus in Capricorn

The most notable trait that comes from Venus in this position is that it makes you trustworthy and able to take on all sorts of responsibilities in life. People are instinctively fond of you and love you all the more because you are always ready to help those who are in any form of need. Social and business popularity can be yours and there is a magnetic quality to your nature that is particularly attractive in a romantic sense. Anyone who wants a partner for a lover, a spouse and a good friend too would almost certainly look in your direction. Constancy is the hallmark of your nature and unfaithfulness would go right against the grain. You might sometimes be a little too trusting.

Venus in Aquarius

This location of Venus offers a fondness for travel and a desire to try out something new at every possible opportunity. You are extremely easy to get along with and tend to have many friends from varied backgrounds, classes and inclinations. You like to live a distinct sort of life and gain a great deal from moving about, both in a career sense and with regard to your home. It is not out of the question that you could form a romantic attachment to someone who comes from far away or be attracted to a person of a distinctly artistic and original nature. What you cannot stand is jealousy, for you have friends of both sexes and would want to keep things that way.

Venus in Pisces

The first thing people tend to notice about you is your wonderful, warm smile. Being very charitable by nature you will do anything to help others, even if you don't know them well. Much of your life may be spent sorting out situations for other people, but it is very important to feel that you are living for yourself too. In the main, you remain cheerful, and tend to be quite attractive to members of the opposite sex. Where romantic attachments are concerned, you could be drawn to people who are significantly older or younger than yourself or to someone with a unique career or point of view. It might be best for you to avoid marrying whilst you are still very young.

CAPRICORN: 2016 DIARY PAGES

October

2016

1 SATURDAY

Moon Age Day 1   Moon Sign Libra

If you are a weekend worker you can now expect a boost to your working conditions or at the very least an improvement in the way you view them. Capricorn people who have the day to themselves may decide that they will take advantage of any fine weather that is still around. The season of mists and mellow fruitfulness is well underway.

2 SUNDAY

Moon Age Day 2   Moon Sign Libra

Keep amongst familiar faces if you can today because mixing too much with strangers could bring a few potential problems at the moment. You have what it takes to make a good impression and could reap some rewards in a romantic sense. Avoid family arguments, particularly as you are not the person starting them.

3 MONDAY

Moon Age Day 3   Moon Sign Scorpio

You should find work and all practical matters to be a real joy. When others are falling by the wayside through boredom or fatigue, you keep going happily. Capricorn has a tremendous ability to stick at a job and this is part of what gets you noticed. Anything old or odd attracts your attention today.

4 TUESDAY

Moon Age Day 4   Moon Sign Scorpio

It is possible that at this time you will find yourself to be under some unexpected pressure, maybe coming from the direction of your family. You need to be quite relaxed about situations and also willing to enlist a little support if you feel you might be out of your depth. In other respects this should be a fairly happy sort of day.

5 WEDNESDAY *Moon Age Day 5 Moon Sign Scorpio*

The emphasis of life turns towards partnerships and in particular towards romantic attachments. Now is the time to think in pairs if you want to be really happy and present trends are also good for partnerships of a more practical nature. Don't be too rushed and allow others to take some of the strain.

6 THURSDAY *Moon Age Day 6 Moon Sign Sagittarius*

You won't want anything to hamper your personal freedom today and if there is any problem at all it will stem from the fact that you feel in some way restricted. Constant attention to detail could so easily get on your nerves at present, which is why the more you diversify, the happier you are likely to be.

7 FRIDAY *Moon Age Day 7 Moon Sign Sagittarius*

Look forward to receiving a favourable response from others and the possibility of a new love developing if that is what you are looking for. Avoid arguments that are not of your making but if you have no choice but to become involved, make sure you win! Pointless rules and regulations could be an irritant, as is often the case for Capricorn.

8 SATURDAY *Moon Age Day 8 Moon Sign Capricorn*

Positive trends are in operation at this time and it shouldn't be at all difficult for you to make significant headway in life generally. What counts the most is your present enthusiasm and your determination to get on well, even though you might have to overcome a few problems on the way.

9 SUNDAY *Moon Age Day 9 Moon Sign Capricorn*

Trends suggest you could make some hasty moves today, but in the main you remain extremely positive and won't let minor irritations get you down too much. Progress is definitely possible if you work at the weekend and it could be the case that you are facing new and exciting responsibilities before very long. Listen to what friends are saying.

10 MONDAY *Moon Age Day 10 Moon Sign Capricorn*

When it comes to getting things done it's clear that you are striking out on your own now. Not all planetary influences are on your side and a good deal of hard work is called for. Constant attention to detail is fine for a few hours but it's essential that you also find ways to relax by the end of the day.

11 TUESDAY *Moon Age Day 11 Moon Sign Aquarius*

Practical pressures are reduced and it isn't at all difficult to do several jobs at the same time, mainly because you are so relaxed about everything. If you find that you have spare time on your hands, indulge your creative side in some way. There are financial gains to be made if you remain shrewd.

12 WEDNESDAY *Moon Age Day 12 Moon Sign Aquarius*

Unexpected assistance is probably what counts the most at this time. All in all you can expect a fairly progressive sort of day but there are little upsets for the unwary. You can't trust everyone and that's something of a problem at a time when you want to give the whole world the clear benefit of the doubt.

13 THURSDAY *Moon Age Day 13 Moon Sign Pisces*

Some high spots in life are evident and today ought to be especially good in a romantic sense. You are filled with a desire to please people and on the way you manage to please yourself as well. As is often the case for Capricorn you find that expected routines are reassuring and give you a sense of solidity.

14 FRIDAY *Moon Age Day 14 Moon Sign Pisces*

Getting through jobs at lightning speed today, you buy yourself the right to relax later, though whether you will bother even then remains to be seen. The fact is that you are looking for excitement and seem to find it around every corner. Small steps taken at this time can have a tremendous bearing on your life later.

15 SATURDAY *Moon Age Day 15 Moon Sign Aries*

You should be firmly in the social mainstream today and it might occur to you that there isn't really all that much time for work or responsibility. Actually, you are doing yourself a great deal of good by simply socialising. Something you did some time ago could now come back to reward you.

16 SUNDAY *Moon Age Day 16 Moon Sign Aries*

You need strong encouragement from others today and that might not be forthcoming. Nevertheless you have what it takes to go solo and although you might be rather nervous about the prospect you will do fine. Ahead is a time during which you constantly learn more about your resources and your willpower.

17 MONDAY *Moon Age Day 17 Moon Sign Taurus*

Compromise is needed if you are going to avoid ego-centred arguments with others. Even if those around you seem unreasonable there is no reason for you to be so. In most situations at present you have what it takes to take the initiative, even when it comes to being the best diplomat.

18 TUESDAY *Moon Age Day 18 Moon Sign Taurus*

Today's sources of joy and pleasure are diverse and you know how to turn heads when it matters the most. Colleagues should be friendly and amusing so you should be getting on well at work. If you are presently in full-time education you can expect to make significant progress at the moment.

19 WEDNESDAY *Moon Age Day 19 Moon Sign Gemini*

Beware of distractions today, especially those that take you away from jobs you know you should be doing. Although planetary trends are still generally good you won't have quite the ability to command life that has been the case recently and may need to concentrate more on specifics in order to succeed.

20 THURSDAY *Moon Age Day 20 Moon Sign Gemini*

Look for things upon which you can capitalise. You should be enjoying the cut and thrust of this busy and enterprising period and will want to get as much change and diversity into your life as possible. A few Capricorn people will even be looking for some kind of adventure to pep up their lives even more.

21 FRIDAY *Moon Age Day 21 Moon Sign Cancer*

Certain personal involvements may prove to be something of a disappointment today and for this you can blame the lunar low. Keep as low a profile as necessary and don't take on new jobs until Sunday. You can gain a great deal from simply sitting on the riverbank of life and watching the water flow.

22 SATURDAY *Moon Age Day 22 Moon Sign Cancer*

Expect the unexpected today – especially in relation to setbacks at work. Once again the rule is not to take on anything new but to wait for a day until trends improve. Keep life simple and enjoy the fact that others seem so willing to do things on your behalf. Don't be too critical of family members or friends.

23 SUNDAY *Moon Age Day 23 Moon Sign Leo*

Because you are now willing to do much in the way of hard work, the rewards that come your way are commensurately greater. Sunday might mean a rest from working routines but you are still likely to find plenty that will keep you busy. Friends push to get your attention so spare them at least a little time.

24 MONDAY *Moon Age Day 24 Moon Sign Leo*

The planets favour contact with influential people at the moment, so keep lines of communication with them open. You could achieve more with one significant conversation than you could with weeks of work. What you are feeling at the moment is also what you are inclined to say and people generally will respect you for your honesty.

25 TUESDAY *Moon Age Day 25 Moon Sign Leo*

Be as sensitive as you can to the moods of other people because to show concern at the moment is going to benefit all concerned in the longer-term. It's a little like taking a driving test. You know you have been looking in the rear-view mirror but you have to demonstrate the fact to the person by your side. Make a good show of everything.

26 WEDNESDAY *Moon Age Day 26 Moon Sign Virgo*

This is no time to stand at the edge of situations looking on. Dipping your toe in the water is only going to make you more nervous. Launch yourself at life and everything will come good for you. Making up your mind as you go along is not always your way but it seems to work at present.

27 THURSDAY *Moon Age Day 27 Moon Sign Virgo*

Stay out there in the social mainstream and at the same time give yourself fully to new projects that you know are going to benefit your life in the medium-term. When it comes to romance you are in the best possible position to please your partner or to get a new relationships started at any time now.

28 FRIDAY *Moon Age Day 28 Moon Sign Libra*

The sorts of people to whom you are attracted right now are those who don't stop to think. Although you cannot be this way yourself you are carried away by a wave of enthusiasm that comes from their direction. However, they need your steadiness just as much as you latch on to their excitement.

29 SATURDAY *Moon Age Day 29 Moon Sign Libra*

Get rid of some non-essentials today and concentrate on those matters that you know are going to be important in the days ahead. You should have more time to concentrate on your love life and will be doing all you can to lift the spirits of people you know well who are having a hard time at the moment.

30 SUNDAY *Moon Age Day 0 Moon Sign Libra*

Don't assume that things are going wrong just because you can't control everything around you. Capricorn hates to be too reliant on others but there are occasions when this proves to be absolutely necessary. A few small struggles are character-building but you can help yourself no end by simply accepting some assistance.

31 MONDAY *Moon Age Day 1 Moon Sign Scorpio*

This is a favourable time to be out and about amongst those you count as your peers. Doubtless you will be constantly called upon for your opinions and advice and as a result it appears that you are enjoying the very end of the month. There are new responsibilities but you should take these in your stride.

November 2016

1 TUESDAY *Moon Age Day 2 Moon Sign Scorpio*

Financial decisions should turn out to be rather more profitable than you might have been thinking or expecting. Take advantage of the good nature of friends and colleagues because they really do want to help you all they can at the moment. Avoid a very slight tendency towards cynicism at this time.

2 WEDNESDAY *Moon Age Day 3 Moon Sign Sagittarius*

This may be one of the best days of the month for social encounters but of course this won't be the case if you have something to do from the moment you get up until the time you crawl back into bed exhausted. Even if it means putting a few jobs on the back burner for a while, you need a few hours to just be you.

3 THURSDAY *Moon Age Day 4 Moon Sign Sagittarius*

You should see an improvement in personal relationships, particularly if things have been a bit strained of late. This is an excellent day for joint ventures of any kind and you will probably be getting on better with people who seem to have been a little difficult to deal with in the recent past.

4 FRIDAY *Moon Age Day 5 Moon Sign Sagittarius*

A boost to all communication matters can be expected now and with the weekend in view you will want to socialise and make plans for outings or gatherings at home. Entertaining people really appeals around this time and you could be showing your cooking skills. Friends are very responsive at the moment.

5 SATURDAY *Moon Age Day 6 Moon Sign Capricorn*

You really should have luck on your side today and can get away with just about anything. A little cheek goes a long way and you make the best possible impression on the world at large. If you have been thinking about a change of job, this might be a good time to either look more closely or to actually take the plunge.

6 SUNDAY *Moon Age Day 7 Moon Sign Capricorn*

The lunar high is certainly an energy-booster and offers you the chance to make progress in a number of different directions. You enjoy an easy confidence, not least of all when you are in social or romantic situations. If you've been wishing to pop the question or to encourage your partner to do so, this could be the time!

7 MONDAY *Moon Age Day 8 Moon Sign Aquarius*

It looks as though you are going to be sought after this week, both professionally and socially. Things are lining up nicely and the only possible problem at present is that you have too much to do. There are people about who strike you as being totally mad but nevertheless you are inclined to join in with them.

8 TUESDAY *Moon Age Day 9 Moon Sign Aquarius*

Conflict could be hard to avoid in personal attachments and it's important to use self-control. It doesn't really matter who is wrong and who is right, simply refuse to argue. In a professional sense you should be getting on better and may be able to make the sort of impression that really counts with superiors.

9 WEDNESDAY *Moon Age Day 10 Moon Sign Pisces*

Planetary influences now turn your attention to private emotional issues. These ought to prove fairly heart-warming and very reassuring. In practical issues you need to keep your eye on the ball. There's someone around at present who really doesn't have too much of a vested interest in seeing you succeed.

10 THURSDAY *Moon Age Day 11 Moon Sign Pisces*

Partnerships and social matters are well highlighted at present and should prove to be the most rewarding area of your life for the moment. Concern for the underdog is very strong around now and you will be happy to argue on behalf of someone you think is being wronged. Take care not to tangle with nasty types, though.

11 FRIDAY *Moon Age Day 12 Moon Sign Pisces*

This really is the right time to be considering what can be done to unblock your life and to get rid of elements of it you don't care for any more. You need to look ahead to fresh starts and can easily win others round with your present cheerful nature. Confidence is everything when you are socialising.

12 SATURDAY *Moon Age Day 13 Moon Sign Aries*

In terms of your career this can be a challenging sort of day but of course it's entirely possible that this being a Saturday you are at home. Get your thinking cap on because there are things you would like to do in the not so distant future that can begin quite soon. Family members should be friendlier than ever this weekend.

13 SUNDAY *Moon Age Day 14 Moon Sign Aries*

All your best qualities are now on display and others may feel almost magnetically attracted to you. It appears that the world is your oyster and don't forget that some oysters contain precious pearls. You won't get too far if you show any lack of confidence in yourself, so get cracking and prove what you are worth.

14 MONDAY *Moon Age Day 15 Moon Sign Taurus*

There is plenty of useful information about at the moment but you need to be in the best possible position to both register this and to do something about it. There's no time to hang around in the background if you really want to get on. Be where the action is – even if the action is scary!

15 TUESDAY *Moon Age Day 16 Moon Sign Taurus*

Today you should find that you are especially well liked by those who employ you and by the people with whom you work. There are possible gains on the financial front, even if these are likely to be of a fairly small nature. Social and romantic opportunities abound, and some of these could well be a surprise.

16 WEDNESDAY *Moon Age Day 17 Moon Sign Gemini*

Your personal life might best be described as inconsistent today and there won't be the hearts and roses that may have been present yesterday. This might not have anything to do with your own attitude or actions and in most senses today you will find that you are reacting to the actions of others.

17 THURSDAY *Moon Age Day 18 Moon Sign Gemini*

This is a time of heightened sensitivity to the needs of those around you. Although you may not feel that you are absolutely in charge of your own life, you are taking the initiative and that is what suits you best. Social arrangements are inclined to be complicated at best and may need some extra attention.

18 FRIDAY *Moon Age Day 19 Moon Sign Cancer*

You can't expect to please all the people all of the time, and with the lunar low around you probably can't please anyone at all. It's possible you are trying too hard, at a time you should be taking a rest. If someone specific chooses to sulk it's probably best just to wait for them to come round.

19 SATURDAY *Moon Age Day 20 Moon Sign Cancer*

This really is a period during which you need to take careful steps and not a time to let go of your self-control. It would be very easy to allow emotion to take over and as a result lose your composure. By tomorrow the lunar low is out of the way but for now just put on the brakes a little and wait.

20 SUNDAY *Moon Age Day 21 Moon Sign Leo*

This is an ideal day during which to express yourself and you will also be taking great note of what other people have to say. Even the most casual remarks coming at you can carry a great significance and should spur you on to different sorts of actions in the days ahead. Romance looks more settled now.

21 MONDAY *Moon Age Day 22 Moon Sign Leo*

Some Capricorn people are likely to be feeling the pangs of nostalgia around this time. It isn't really like you to look back too much because you have a fairly hard edge and tend to realise that it is the present and future that counts. Nevertheless, today you will think about the past and maybe feel a little regret.

22 TUESDAY *Moon Age Day 23 Moon Sign Virgo*

All of a sudden you could be surrounded by surprises, some of which should suit you no end. Reacting on the spur of the moment might not be easy under prevailing trends but if you want to make the most of what life has on offer you should do your best to accept what is happening around you.

23 WEDNESDAY *Moon Age Day 24 Moon Sign Virgo*

This has the potential to be one of the best days for romance that you will experience during the whole of November. It really depends on the way you react and whether or not you take the remarks of others seriously. Try to do this and not worry about getting yourself in some emotional hot water.

24 THURSDAY *Moon Age Day 25 Moon Sign Libra*

In many ways you now seem to want results too soon and this is quite unusual for steady Capricorn. Maybe it is at home that things are not working out quite the way you would wish and a little more patience could be necessary. Friends offer an antidote to routine, so have a good time socially.

25 FRIDAY *Moon Age Day 26 Moon Sign Libra*

You are likely to be quite efficient today and definitely in the mood for organising things. That's fine as far as your own life is concerned but you could discover that colleagues or friends are quite happy to do things their own way. A little give and take is needed and most of it should come from you today.

26 SATURDAY *Moon Age Day 27 Moon Sign Libra*

In a social sense you tend to get what you want today simply by being in the right place at the right time. Some would call this luck but there is more to it for the average Capricorn individual. Romance rears its head both now and tomorrow and you will definitely be interested.

27 SUNDAY *Moon Age Day 28 Moon Sign Scorpio*

Now you can more successfully advance your aspirations for the future. If you don't work at the weekend spend time with your thinking head on, working out how best to approach situations next week. You remain socially motivated and might really enjoy a shopping spree in the company of friends.

28 MONDAY *Moon Age Day 29 Moon Sign Scorpio*

There is the possibility of some real high spots today, mainly because of your own state of mind. Most Capricorns will be bright and breezy, happy to try something new and keen to get on well with everyone. New starts are indicated and these may see you trying a completely new approach in some way.

29 TUESDAY *Moon Age Day 0 Moon Sign Sagittarius*

You are now in a peace-loving mood and won't be inclined to cross swords with anyone if you can avoid doing so. The day is neutral and that might make some aspects of your life seem a little tedious. What is needed are some social high-spots and the chance to express yourself amongst people you like.

30 WEDNESDAY *Moon Age Day 1 Moon Sign Sagittarius*

Keep the demands you make of others to a minimum and wherever possible do things for yourself. The fact is that you could become slightly unpopular if you push too much and in any case you will be more successful when relying on your own skills. Routines should seem somehow comfortable at the moment.

December

2016

1 THURSDAY *Moon Age Day 2 Moon Sign Sagittarius*

Be careful at present because it would be so easy to misread the messages that are coming from your partner, or even a good friend. You are usually quite good at reading people's inner mind but that ability has left you for the moment. Maybe you need to ask some leading questions instead.

2 FRIDAY *Moon Age Day 3 Moon Sign Capricorn*

This is basically a time when the tide of good fortune is running in your favour. You would be slightly mad not to make the best of opportunities that naturally come your way and you can have a strong influence on the way those around you are behaving. Make a real fuss of your partner and family members today.

3 SATURDAY *Moon Age Day 4 Moon Sign Capricorn*

It seems that on this particular day you have everything going for you and any early Christmas parties are likely to be much more fun than you might have expected. With tremendous energy you are a powerhouse of possibilities. All the same it might be necessary to allow others to catch up.

4 SUNDAY *Moon Age Day 5 Moon Sign Aquarius*

You find that matters associated with security make you feel more settled than of late. The planetary picture is now starting to be much more helpful and that's got to be good. Others find you especially attractive at this time and probably won't be shy when it comes to telling you so.

5 MONDAY *Moon Age Day 6 Moon Sign Aquarius*

In very small ways this may not be the most stable time of the month, if only because you are a little nervy for unaccountable reasons. You might be running away with the idea that some fairly sweeping changes are in the offing. Don't worry because when the time comes the choices will be yours.

6 TUESDAY *Moon Age Day 7 Moon Sign Aquarius*

An in-depth chat would be good today, together with a slight withdrawal from competitive situations. Instead of crossing swords with anyone, be determined to simply have fun. You don't want to take yourself or anyone very seriously and at least you are not quite so likely to be let down today.

7 WEDNESDAY *Moon Age Day 8 Moon Sign Pisces*

This is not a time during which you would easily be dissuaded from your personal plans and desires. You might already be in the party spirit but you ought to exercise a little self-control. It's good for people to enjoy themselves but Capricorn sometimes finds the means to enjoy itself a little too much.

8 THURSDAY *Moon Age Day 9 Moon Sign Pisces*

A joint financial matter involving a friend or colleague could mean that you are on the losing end if you are not scrupulous in the way you handle your finances today. Keep up your efforts to help bring a very special Christmas to someone who has not had the best of life in the recent past. Don't get carried away with commercialism.

9 FRIDAY *Moon Age Day 10 Moon Sign Aries*

Bear in mind that a sense of freedom is the key to your genuine happiness at the moment. Today's sources of pleasure should have a distinctly cultural quality and you will be especially happy if you can spend time with those who are refined or who have good taste. Devote the evening to family matters.

10 SATURDAY *Moon Age Day 11 Moon Sign Aries*

Talks and negotiations, whilst quite amicable today, may find you settling for too little. Better by far to aim well above your expectations and then you can't be disappointed. Not everyone is as trustworthy as you would wish right now, even if it's not really their fault. You need to be just a little cautious.

11 SUNDAY *Moon Age Day 12 Moon Sign Taurus*

Certain influences at home could distract you from what is going on in the practical world. Your confidence is high enough but you might lack quite the level of support from people on whom you should be able to rely. If you get bored with doing the same things repeatedly, find ways to make changes.

12 MONDAY *Moon Age Day 13 Moon Sign Taurus*

Events taking place in the outside world lift your spirits now and give you the chance to push ahead with ever-greater optimism. There might be the odd awkward person to deal with but in the main you are coming across people who are more than willing to lend a hand when it is necessary.

13 TUESDAY *Moon Age Day 14 Moon Sign Gemini*

As long as you are careful not to try to arrange everyone today you should have a generally good time. You have a very definite urge at the moment to get everything right, which is fine as long as it is restricted to you. On the other hand you could try to be more casual and enjoy the day even more.

14 WEDNESDAY *Moon Age Day 15 Moon Sign Gemini*

It is likely that you will be quite ambitious and anxious to make a positive impression on the world at large. This is a good time to show off your leadership skills and you should find that others are quite willing to follow your lead. Romance will also be uppermost in your mind.

15 THURSDAY *Moon Age Day 16 Moon Sign Cancer*

Getting ahead today might prove to be a little difficult but don't worry too much because the lunar low won't be especially potent this time around. It's more likely to be the case that you will simply be selective about what you choose to do, leaving others to take a bit more of the strain than normal.

16 FRIDAY *Moon Age Day 17 Moon Sign Cancer*

Another slightly lack-lustre day but you remain anxious to get ahead, especially on the romantic front. If there's a party to go to, you will be there, lunar low or not. Some Capricorn people could be suffering from minor headaches or stress pains of one sort or another. Loosen up as much as you can because that's the best medicine.

17 SATURDAY *Moon Age Day 18 Moon Sign Leo*

A social contract of some sort could prove to be a disappointment and you may have to alter your plans at the last minute. If you are willing to do so, you could have a better time than ever. This only goes to show that flexibility is a good thing – something the average Capricorn is inclined to forget.

18 SUNDAY *Moon Age Day 19 Moon Sign Leo*

There could be a slight downside to loving relationships right now, maybe because you find it slightly difficult to tell people exactly how you feel. For Capricorns who are not committed to a permanent relationship, this might not be the best time of the month to make a new commitment, at least not without some thought.

19 MONDAY *Moon Age Day 20 Moon Sign Virgo*

Life has probably not been as busy for a number of weeks as it is right now. This is the last week in the run-up to Christmas and you will want to get a few practical or professional jobs out of the way as soon as you can. In addition, you will almost certainly have a hectic social schedule ahead of you.

20 TUESDAY ☿ *Moon Age Day 21 Moon Sign Virgo*

Today should be quite fulfilling on the domestic front but you will have to work that bit harder to get on the right side of genuinely awkward types. It could be that you have failed to understand just how strongly someone feels about an issue that is of no real importance to you. It is important to listen.

21 WEDNESDAY ☿ *Moon Age Day 22 Moon Sign Virgo*

The feelings of people around you at present are somewhat difficult to interpret so once again you will have to concentrate and to really listen to what is being said. There ought to be time for reflection and a greater desire than ever to get things right. Thoughts of Christmas will doubtless also occupy your mind.

22 THURSDAY ☿ *Moon Age Day 23 Moon Sign Libra*

Your intellectual powers are good and there is now much to be gained from listening to some new input. Keep busy and active and don't get so bogged down with plans for Christmas that you fail to recognise the opportunities around you now that have nothing to do with the festivities.

23 FRIDAY ☿ *Moon Age Day 24 Moon Sign Libra*

When it comes to financial issues and general family arrangements you will probably be in your element today. Your organisational skills are second to none and you show everyone how cheerful and happy you can be. This might be the most contented day of the whole of the Christmas period.

24 SATURDAY ☿ *Moon Age Day 25 Moon Sign Scorpio*

Even though it is Christmas Eve you could require a little self-control, although if you are able to conquer those little hurdles in your own mind you could push forward positively into new areas of life. The results of today really depend on whether you feel obliged to apply the brakes or just freewheel.

25 SUNDAY ☿ *Moon Age Day 26 Moon Sign Scorpio*

In case it had not occurred to you, this is Christmas Day! Pull out all the stops to widen the angle you have on life and make this day special for everyone. The less you concentrate on your own needs, the better it will turn out to be. This is the very best of Capricorn: kind, concerned and extremely loving.

26 MONDAY ☿ *Moon Age Day 27 Moon Sign Scorpio*

Avoid dwelling too much on personal issues from the past. It might be Boxing Day, but for some reason you are too nostalgic for your own good. As has been the case throughout much of this year you have to realise that what is gone cannot be regained and if the truth is faced you wouldn't want it to be.

27 TUESDAY ☿ *Moon Age Day 28 Moon Sign Sagittarius*

Your present chances of success could hardly be better. There is only one thing that might get in the way and that's likely to be the holiday period. The enforced break might be problem, which is why you have to work that much harder now in order to be able to take the time you also need to enjoy yourself.

28 WEDNESDAY ☿ *Moon Age Day 29 Moon Sign Sagittarius*

Let loved ones know how you really feel about things and don't be afraid to tell it the way it is. People generally will respect you for your honesty and will be likely to follow your lead as a result. This would be a good day for a shopping spree or for committing yourself to one large purchase.

29 THURSDAY ☿ *Moon Age Day 0 Moon Sign Capricorn*

The bigger your ambitions, the better they are now likely to work out. With the lunar high giving you a firm push you need to be working as hard as you can to gain your objectives. Energy levels are likely to be particularly good, and you may have a positive response to a suggestion from others.

30 FRIDAY ☿ *Moon Age Day 1 Moon Sign Capricorn*

It is just possible that you will run out of steam before the end of the day but you will be able to look back at a period that is almost certain to have been both interesting and productive. Take a well-earned rest in the evening. Tomorrow is another day and you will need all the energy that remains.

31 SATURDAY ☿ *Moon Age Day 2 Moon Sign Capricorn*

There is no doubt that you love to be with friends and will now probably be feeling increasingly less intense than has been the case for a day or two. You should have a greater willingness to let your hair down. Nobody is dafter than Capricorn when the private restrictions you place around yourself are released.

CAPRICORN: 2017 DIARY PAGES

CAPRICORN: YOUR YEAR IN BRIEF

You are starting out as you mean to go on so keep up your early efforts during January and February to make something of yourself this year. No effort is wasted in your desire to get ahead and your generally pleasant mood at this time can be used to your advantage in all sorts of ways. Good things from the past may also re-visit you now. This would be a good time to make up your mind about potential changes within your home.

In March and April, the arrival of the spring finds you on top form and very keen to get ahead whenever circumstances allow. Focusing a lot on matters of the heart, you should pay more attention to family and friends. Any money that comes your way now is likely to be as much as a result of luck as good planning on your behalf.

May and June bring some generally favourable trends, even if there are a few delays and small disappointments to deal with too. None of these should hold you up for long and you are so good at working through or round potential pitfalls that you may not even notice them. All the same this may not be the best time for financial risks or for pushing yourself too hard. In terms of your personal life you may be taking time out to look at relationships in a fresh and interesting way.

The arrival of the midsummer period sees you confident and very sociable, which is essential for sometimes reserved Capricorn. Your friendly ways now stand you in good stead, but watch out for those who would seek to part you from your money. July offers some scope for travel, though August is far better and also brings quite radical changes to your way of thinking.

In September and October you should be willing to pause for a period and to watch what's going on around you. It isn't that you have stopped moving forward at all, merely that you are consolidating your position in life. In a selfless mood, you will be offering a great deal of help to others at this stage. People always love you, but are likely to be even warmer towards you at this stage of the year. Trends suggest that you should give some thought to alterations at home and get on with these before the end of the year.

The last two months of a generally busy year, November and December, are replete with opportunities, many of which come like a bolt from the blue. In the main, you are responding to actions you took earlier in the year. You may have to look back in order to move forward but your presently innovative mind is on the move, especially during the Christmas period and on towards the New Year.

January

2017

1 SUNDAY ☿ *Moon Age Day 4 Moon Sign Aquarius*

You may need to face up to the fact that a few white lies will be necessary if you really want to get your own way today. This sort of behaviour doesn't come at all easily to you, though there are planetary trends around that can help. Anything really old or distinctly curious is apt to appeal to you during the week ahead.

2 MONDAY ☿ *Moon Age Day 5 Moon Sign Aquarius*

There probably won't be a great deal of spare time today. Life is busy and you feel a good deal of pressure being placed upon your shoulders. You can deal with this so much better if you are prepared for it. Issues you don't understand may take you by surprise so try to avoid them if at all possible.

3 TUESDAY ☿ *Moon Age Day 6 Moon Sign Pisces*

Work hard at your efforts to gain materially but also take a look at romance, which appears potentially very good at present. Young or young-at-heart Capricorns can gain much from present planetary trends. You might find it somewhat difficult to tell a friend exactly what you think, but it may be necessary to do so diplomatically at some point.

4 WEDNESDAY ☿ *Moon Age Day 7 Moon Sign Pisces*

Even when others make it very clear that you are wrong, you are unlikely to change either your stance or your actions unless they prove a point to you. You have plenty of energy to spare so it would be sensible to do any jobs and tasks you can today, and avoid putting things off until a later date.

5 THURSDAY ☿ *Moon Age Day 8 Moon Sign Aries*

Make sure you stay well away from get-rich-quick schemes today. Your intuition tells you that there is a good chance you will get your fingers burned and there isn't much doubt that this could be the case. A new hobby could be up your street at the moment, especially if it is one that has a physical dimension, so turn your attentions in this direction instead.

6 FRIDAY ☿ *Moon Age Day 9 Moon Sign Aries*

Friday could bring a slight change of pace, or at least an alteration to the way you view your life. Slower and steadier now, you may decide that you need to spend more time in the bosom of your family, enjoying the comforts that this can bring. Failing this, you could be looking up friends you haven't seen for quite a while.

7 SATURDAY ☿ *Moon Age Day 10 Moon Sign Taurus*

Keep up the pressure in professional matters if you are a weekend worker. If this isn't the case, turn your attention to finding ways to enjoy yourself. Most Capricorns like to keep busy and with trends favouring your creative potential at the moment, it isn't out of the question that you will be decorating your home or helping with projects at a friend's house.

8 SUNDAY *Moon Age Day 11 Moon Sign Taurus*

There are times when maximum effort is necessary and other periods when it is far preferable to take things slowly and steadily. Your deeper thought processes are working really well on this Sunday, so mull situations over carefully. If necessary, enlist the direct intervention of a friend to help with your plans and schemes.

9 MONDAY *Moon Age Day 12 Moon Sign Gemini*

If you get the impression that anyone is playing games with you today, it is important to make your feelings known. Social trends are good and tend to draw you out of yourself, though this will probably not take effect until somewhat later in the day. Finances should strengthen under prevailing trends.

10 TUESDAY *Moon Age Day 13 Moon Sign Gemini*

This might be a day for making lists. Specific planetary trends incline you to be more absent-minded than would normally be the case. Just as long as you review matters early in the day, and avoid forgetting anything important, you will proceed normally. Family gatherings are distinctly possible at present.

11 WEDNESDAY *Moon Age Day 14 Moon Sign Cancer*

This is likely to be a quieter day and one that works better with contemplation, instead of action. Do your best to take life steadily, watching from the banks as the river of life flows by. It might seem rather non-productive but at the end of the day, you function better when you have time to think.

12 THURSDAY *Moon Age Day 15 Moon Sign Cancer*

Things are still likely to be slow but don't let this worry you because these trends certainly will not last long. Confidence is not especially high, that is unless you enlist the support of people you really know well and trust. Spend some time with family members and find the right words to tell them how much you care.

13 FRIDAY *Moon Age Day 16 Moon Sign Cancer*

Little unexpected gains are there for the taking. You won't become a millionaire today, but if you keep your wits about you there is a possibility you could take the first step. You are never anyone's fool but at the moment your perceptions are razor sharp. Don't be afraid to rely on your intuition when assessing others.

14 SATURDAY *Moon Age Day 17 Moon Sign Leo*

Enjoy whatever delights the weekend has to offer. Yours is a winter-born sign and so the cold weather doesn't bother you much. It's a fact that many Capricorns will be finding ways and means to take a break of some sort at any time now. This is especially likely to be the case if you worked through Christmas.

15 SUNDAY *Moon Age Day 18 Moon Sign Leo*

You could be very motivated today, especially during the afternoon and evening. If you are feeling a surge of wanderlust, now is the time to exploit that fact by taking a journey, whether long or short. Don't be too quick to judge younger family members, no matter how they seem to be behaving. There may be more to the situation than meets the eye.

16 MONDAY *Moon Age Day 19 Moon Sign Virgo*

You might have to give in a little to the opinions and ideas of others today, even if to do so goes against the grain. In the end, you will only accept this when you realise that in the longer term you will gain from this action. As always Capricorn tends to look far ahead and is willing to sacrifice now in order to get ahead eventually.

17 TUESDAY *Moon Age Day 20 Moon Sign Virgo*

Personal relationships might not seem to be all that inspiring at the moment but there are things you can do to alter this state of affairs. Perhaps all that is really needed is a slight change of attitude on your part. It is possible that you are holding on to a point of view that really doesn't stand up to the scrutiny of today.

18 WEDNESDAY *Moon Age Day 21 Moon Sign Libra*

Private matters are likely to occupy your mind a great deal at present, though there is some sense of fulfilment when you manage to achieve objectives that have eluded you previously. It would be generally sensible to keep a low profile when in public situations and not to say too much unless you feel really confident.

19 THURSDAY *Moon Age Day 22 Moon Sign Libra*

Be careful about believing everything you hear today, if only because there are people around who appear to have a definite interest in diverting you from the truth. Check out any attractive-sounding proposals very carefully. There is a good chance that at least some of these are not at all what they first appear to be.

20 FRIDAY *Moon Age Day 23 Moon Sign Scorpio*

You are now likely to embark on projects that have been on the back burner for quite some time and may be able to influence the decisions made by others. Any tendency to lethargy over the last few days is now definitely out of the window and you are heading towards a generally more energetic phase.

21 SATURDAY *Moon Age Day 24 Moon Sign Scorpio*

Don't be too bigheaded about anything today. There is always the chance that those around you could misconstrue what you are trying to say – and why. It's time to explain what you mean fully and to make the most of the support that comes from particularly good friends. Keep away from arguments altogether.

22 SUNDAY *Moon Age Day 25 Moon Sign Scorpio*

The wheels of progress keep turning on, sometimes even despite the fact that you don't seem to be contributing too much. Financially it appears that you are now dealing with situations one at a time. Capricorn is coming into its own, especially when making decisions proves to be particularly important.

23 MONDAY *Moon Age Day 26 Moon Sign Sagittarius*

Capricorn will not shy away from any sort of challenge that comes along on this particular day. Getting what you want from life isn't at all difficult right now and there should be plenty of support around if you are in the market for it. Friends may occasionally have their own agenda but you can cope with that.

24 TUESDAY *Moon Age Day 27 Moon Sign Sagittarius*

You probably won't be feeling on top of the world but that is only really because the Moon is now in your solar twelfth house. Things look better if you concentrate on home-based issues and if you leave practical and professional situations until later. Intuition is important so don't rely entirely on logic.

25 WEDNESDAY *Moon Age Day 28 Moon Sign Capricorn*

The Moon is in your zodiac sign, bringing the lunar high, that time during each month when you are emotionally and physically motivated. Anything you decide to do today is undertaken with a great deal of enthusiasm and plenty of determination. What's more, you have good luck on your side.

26 THURSDAY *Moon Age Day 29 Moon Sign Capricorn*

The lunar high continues so keep up your efforts! Even things you have had great difficulty doing in the past should come much easier today. If you have to enlist the help and support of friends or colleagues simply turn on the charm. It's doubtful that anyone could turn down a reasonable request from your direction at present.

27 FRIDAY *Moon Age Day 0 Moon Sign Capricorn*

Today marks a time when you can get much enjoyment simply from being amongst familiar faces. Less outgoing than you have been for a couple of days, spending some time on your own might appeal too. A certain degree of bravado is still present for those situations that demand it and you tend to smile a lot.

28 SATURDAY *Moon Age Day 1 Moon Sign Aquarius*

Any sort of travel, together with all intellectual pursuits is well highlighted by present trends. Staying in the same place for too long could prove to be quite tedious and you can gain greatly, simply by keeping your options open and moving around freely. A more free and easy sort of Capricorn is beginning to show.

29 SUNDAY *Moon Age Day 2 Moon Sign Aquarius*

Present planetary positions bring a potentially busy time and a period when you can gain from the viewpoints of friends and colleagues alike. At present you are able to elicit the best from those around you, many of whom will want to assist you for no reason other than that they like you so much.

30 MONDAY *Moon Age Day 3 Moon Sign Pisces*

Although getting ahead at work might seem to present a few problems, you won't be stuck for some good ideas. Mentally and physically you should now be on a peak and ready to reap some rewards as a result of your past efforts. Capricorn is always much stronger and more robust than it considers itself to be.

31 TUESDAY *Moon Age Day 4 Moon Sign Pisces*

The balance of life is extremely important today, so don't allow yourself to be browbeaten into doing things at home that go against the grain. Change and diversity are important and you will be happier than would usually be the case to mix with newcomers and people who have not been your cup of tea before.

February
2017

1 WEDNESDAY *Moon Age Day 5 Moon Sign Aries*

Something inside you is screaming that you should be putting your point of view forward more strongly, and that is certainly the case at work. If you are looking for a job at the moment, today could be a good time to make further enquiries. There might not be much excitement about, but there is potential gain.

2 THURSDAY *Moon Age Day 6 Moon Sign Aries*

That dry Capricorn humour is still very much in evidence. You have a great ability to make almost anyone laugh today and if there is something you have to complain about, you do so with a joke. Rules and regulations are inclined to get on your nerves right now, that is if you don't simply decide to ignore them altogether.

3 FRIDAY *Moon Age Day 7 Moon Sign Aries*

You have an amazing ability to go straight to the heart of just about any matter now. It would be great if you could decide to take today off work because you are also feeling somewhat hemmed in by responsibility and general circumstances. What you seem to need most of all now is a temporary change of scenery.

4 SATURDAY *Moon Age Day 8 Moon Sign Taurus*

Standing up for your rights and for those of the people you care for seems to be very important at present but so is making sure that there is genuinely something to complain about before you get cracking. Checking details is important in every sphere of your life today and particularly so in travel arrangements.

5 SUNDAY *Moon Age Day 9 Moon Sign Taurus*

Anything to do with modern technology not only attracts you at the moment but also shows how your mind tends to work. You can be incredibly logical right now and arrive at some startling conclusions this weekend as a result. Try to get away from too many family-based domestic routines and strive for something different.

6 MONDAY *Moon Age Day 10 Moon Sign Gemini*

If there is something you don't like today, ignore it. This isn't usually the sort of advice that would be offered to Capricorn but it is highly likely that you are now getting yourself into a state about nothing. Clear your head by taking a long walk and give some thought to long-term changes in your career.

7 TUESDAY *Moon Age Day 11 Moon Sign Gemini*

You are well ahead of the competition in some respects, even though it may appear to you that others are making more progress than you are. A little patience is required, along with some confidence in your own past decisions. There are times during this part of the week when it is vital for you to keep your nerve.

8 WEDNESDAY *Moon Age Day 12 Moon Sign Cancer*

You won't be feeling at your best today, or at least not achieving the number of successes you might wish. For this you can thank the lunar low, though its presence in your life does at least give you the chance to take a break. Avoid family disputes or, if you cannot do so, sort them out quickly.

9 THURSDAY *Moon Age Day 13 Moon Sign Cancer*

You could be somewhat forgetful today and inclined to miss out on one or two things as a result. Don't be too quick to take on extra responsibilities and be willing to wait for successes, which are slow in maturing. Confidence gradually begins to return, though even tomorrow could start slowly.

10 FRIDAY *Moon Age Day 14 Moon Sign Leo*

Some jobs prove to be so complicated you will want to go back to the drawing board and start them again. Although others will disagree, rely on your own intuition in this regard. If you are in a position of some responsibility, those below you could seem to question your decisions generally, which you must not allow.

11 SATURDAY *Moon Age Day 15 Moon Sign Leo*

Now less inclined to look back to past situations, you are gradually growing more confident in your own vision of the future. That cannot be said to be the case for everyone around you, though your persuasive skills could make all the difference. With a little genuine belief, you can have almost anything now.

12 SUNDAY *Moon Age Day 16 Moon Sign Virgo*

You are definitely working at your best in an intellectual sense. You would be especially good at any sort of competitions now and should take things like IQ tests easily in your stride. Maybe you can take a look at yourself and really understand on how many different levels your versatile mind can function.

13 MONDAY *Moon Age Day 17 Moon Sign Virgo*

This might turn out to be potentially one of the most eventful days of February so far. Part of the reason for this lies in the fact that you are making things happen. Your popularity is on the rise, thanks in great part to your more vibrant personality and your off the wall sense of humour. Get out and about and make sure people notice you.

14 TUESDAY *Moon Age Day 18 Moon Sign Libra*

Things may not be happening quite the way you intended, but that doesn't mean they work against your best interests. On this Valentine's Day you should keep a sense of proportion in regard to romance, don't go over the top and don't be surprised if you turn someone's head, even without trying. The charisma of Capricorn is now evident.

15 WEDNESDAY *Moon Age Day 19 Moon Sign Libra*

You can be the life and soul of any party at present. Although Capricorn is one of the quieter signs of the zodiac, when you do choose to turn up the charm, there is nobody better. Don't assume just because a particular situation didn't turn out to your advantage in the past, it will fail to do so again. Persistence is everything.

16 THURSDAY *Moon Age Day 20 Moon Sign Libra*

You now tend to be pushier and always eager to get ahead. Not everyone will behave in quite the way you either expect or plan, which can be the fly in the ointment for some of your schemes. You do, however, have great resilience and won't easily be dissuaded from taking actions you feel to be right.

17 FRIDAY *Moon Age Day 21 Moon Sign Scorpio*

Making profit comes as second nature to Sagittarius and you are especially good at it right now. The Sun is particularly useful around this time and heightens your ability to see a good opportunity or a bargain. If you keep your wits about you now, you can make a stunning purchase and really haggle for an excellent price.

18 SATURDAY *Moon Age Day 22 Moon Sign Scorpio*

Positive influences should now prevail in personal and family matters. You will enjoy the company of certain people enormously and may find yourself once again striking up a relationship that was important to you in the past. Your confidence to get what you want from life remains generally high, aided by your positive attitude.

19 SUNDAY *Moon Age Day 23 Moon Sign Sagittarius*

This particular Sunday should be very lucky for you. This is one of the best days of the month in which to concentrate your effort for better results. This applies to situations that improve your life materially but is equally important when it comes to getting what you need from a personal attachment.

20 MONDAY *Moon Age Day 24 Moon Sign Sagittarius*

The positive trends continue and general good luck pays a potentially important visit to your life. Ignore restraints and push through obstacles. There are plenty of new incentives about, the difference being now that you notice them. Concern for friends who find themselves in a dilemma turns to practical assistance.

21 TUESDAY *Moon Age Day 25 Moon Sign Sagittarius*

You can now take constructive action to expand your financial successes and will use specific situations to feather your own nest. However, you won't be forgetting about the more personal side of life and it looks as though romance could be well to the forefront of your mind at present. There is time for everything if you plan carefully.

22 WEDNESDAY *Moon Age Day 26 Moon Sign Capricorn*

A time of discrimination and organisation is at hand. You see things very clearly today and there are no shades of grey in your life at all. Later in the day you may be overtaken by a more nostalgic frame of mind and could so easily be reliving a few minor regrets left over from the dim and distant past. Don't allow these worries to hold you back.

23 THURSDAY *Moon Age Day 27 Moon Sign Capricorn*

Opportunities should present themselves today for you to communicate your personal ideas with great authority. This is important because even if you don't know exactly what you are talking about, others will never guess that this is the case. Keep up your present efforts to lend assistance to good friends.

24 FRIDAY *Moon Age Day 28 Moon Sign Aquarius*

You could find yourself drawn to expensive and glamorous articles. This happens to everyone now and again but is fairly unusual for Capricorn. A love of luxury is sometimes present in you but is often a response to insecurity. Maybe you need to look at what is happening in and around your personal life?

25 SATURDAY *Moon Age Day 0 Moon Sign Aquarius*

You are able to express yourself with a great deal of conviction today and few people will be left in any doubt whatsoever about the way you are feeling. The attitude of friends can be somewhat puzzling and might lead you to asking a few leading questions in your search to help your pals out of a pickle.

26 SUNDAY *Moon Age Day 1 Moon Sign Aquarius*

You are thoughtful and considerate of the feelings of others, which in turn inclines them to be extra pleasant to you. This is just as likely when you are dealing with strangers as it would be with those you know well. Don't be intimidated if you feel just slightly out of you depth early in the coming week and stick to what you know is right.

27 MONDAY *Moon Age Day 2 Moon Sign Pisces*

There could be something of a conflict between personal desires and your ability to focus your mind on more abstract issues. This won't be too difficult to solve because on a basic level, concentration is easy for you. The demands and expectations of those around you have to be taken into account around now.

28 TUESDAY *Moon Age Day 3 Moon Sign Pisces*

This could be quite a productive day in the financial sphere and a time when you should be feeling safe and secure. You have your own efforts to thank for this state of affairs – together with a little help from your family and friends. It might be good to take the time out today to acknowledge their support.

March 2017

1 WEDNESDAY *Moon Age Day 4 Moon Sign Aries*

Advancement is much more likely today than has been the case since the weekend. You can afford to take some little, well-thought-out chances because all risks for you now are calculated ones. Make the most of this admirable time for romance, when people may be virtually queuing up to tell you how wonderful you are.

2 THURSDAY *Moon Age Day 5 Moon Sign Aries*

There could be a love interest on the horizon for Capricorn, particularly those of you who have been looking for that very special romance. Don't be too quick to jump to conclusions regarding material matters and if you are in any doubt whatsoever opt for a patient attitude and bide your time. Rushing into financial commitments is never a good idea.

3 FRIDAY *Moon Age Day 6 Moon Sign Taurus*

Intimate concerns and domestic situations seem to be your most important priorities around now. At what is probably the end of a working week, you might not be all that happy with the general progress you have made, but take heart from the fact that you have probably done much better overall than you realise.

4 SATURDAY *Moon Age Day 7 Moon Sign Taurus*

In a social sense, you should find plenty of light-hearted moments to pep up today. Work-wise, you are not in such a good position. If you do work today it is possible that colleagues misunderstand your point of view and likewise friends in social situations. Explaining yourself is vital at this time.

5 SUNDAY *Moon Age Day 8 Moon Sign Gemini*

Avoid getting carried away with issues that don't have anything directly to do with your life at present. Retain your energy for really important tasks because although you have plenty of get-up-and-go right now, it is easily dissipated. It's quality rather than quantity that really pays out at this time.

6 MONDAY *Moon Age Day 9 Moon Sign Gemini*

Nothing ventured, nothing gained should be your adage now. Yours is not a zodiac sign that is used to taking too many chances but if you don't do so now, you could be the loser. If you have any doubts seek out the help and advice of a good friend, someone who will point you in the right direction. Avoid any tendency to rush, though, and think things through carefully.

7 TUESDAY *Moon Age Day 10 Moon Sign Cancer*

There could be some stumbling blocks on the path to progress today, whether or not you are working today. The lunar low has the power this time round to sap your resolve somewhat, though if you appreciate what is causing your state of mind, you will be half way to defeating it. Take some time out to spend with your partner or your family.

8 WEDNESDAY *Moon Age Day 11 Moon Sign Cancer*

Some things just refuse to go as you have planned today and there isn't any getting away from the fact. If necessary, you will start again tomorrow and redo whatever went wrong. Rather than allowing this to annoy you, accept that it might not turn out to be a bad thing at all because you may be infinitely more successful second time around.

9 THURSDAY *Moon Age Day 12 Moon Sign Leo*

You are likely to be getting the best from most spheres of life, though the accent is turning towards domestic matters. Relatives may have a special need of you today and you will certainly be willing to help out when you can. Real puzzles are something you might want to mull over for a while.

10 FRIDAY *Moon Age Day 13 Moon Sign Leo*

Planetary trends suggest that you should be registering a genuinely light-hearted period, during which you find the answers you need almost without trying. If you do come up against the odd problem today, there is likely to be someone around who will solve it for you. The difference now is that you are not too shy or retiring to ask.

11 SATURDAY *Moon Age Day 14 Moon Sign Virgo*

Mundane and domestic matters can be trying, which is why you are looking for diversity in your weekend. Your confidence remains generally high, though there are people around who would change that situation if they could. Watch out for someone who wants to throw a spanner in the works and give them a very wide berth indeed.

12 SUNDAY *Moon Age Day 15 Moon Sign Virgo*

Differences of opinion in your vicinity don't really have to have a bearing on the way you behave, especially if you refuse to take a stance. The fact that you won't get involved might slightly annoy others but in the end they will respect you more for remaining neutral. From your diplomatic standpoint you can then play the honest broker.

13 MONDAY *Moon Age Day 16 Moon Sign Virgo*

Turning your attention today towards the professional aspects of life, the wonderful array of different planetary positions helps you no end. Mars, in its present position, is all about efficiency and dealing with matters as and when they arise. There isn't any reason to rush and plenty of assistance is on hand. Begin early on this Monday morning and start as you mean to go on.

14 TUESDAY *Moon Age Day 17 Moon Sign Libra*

Both socially and romantically, there is much to captivate your interest now. It is possible that you are well ahead in your work, which ought to leave time for simply enjoying yourself. Consolidation is one of the most important factors to Capricorns but, for a change, you might find that it is barely of any interest during such a spontaneous phase.

15 WEDNESDAY *Moon Age Day 18 Moon Sign Libra*

This is potentially a time of small but regular increases where finances are concerned. Concentrate your effort in places and situations you know and understand. You have a strong willingness to help others, especially any friends that you know are going through a hard time at the moment.

16 THURSDAY *Moon Age Day 19 Moon Sign Scorpio*

You will take great pleasure in being on the move at the moment. There is no shortage of opportunities for your fertile mind. Flexible, interested and very friendly, you should surge through the day. If not everything is turning out as you wish, heed the fact that maybe this is because you are simply not trying hard enough.

17 FRIDAY *Moon Age Day 20 Moon Sign Scorpio*

What a great day this will be for Capricorn to make the best of any new situation that comes its way. There could be some particularly interesting news regarding recent efforts you have made. Your creative potential is especially good and you are likely to be proud of a particular accomplishment. The weekend ahead might be fun.

18 SATURDAY *Moon Age Day 21 Moon Sign Scorpio*

You are at your best when it comes to socialising today. That's not to suggest that you are failing to do what is necessary in a practical sense. It ought to be possible to mix business with pleasure to a great extent and to offer the best of what Capricorn can be to the world at large and especially to your partner.

19 SUNDAY *Moon Age Day 22 Moon Sign Sagittarius*

Should you feel somewhat under-par today you can take heart from the fact that this is a very temporary phase. You may have to rely a good deal on others, which isn't particularly easy for Capricorn. As long as you don't try to rush your fences, there can still be plenty of enjoyment in the day and some significant rewards.

20 MONDAY *Moon Age Day 23 Moon Sign Sagittarius*

Capricorn has a strong stubborn streak and will only do what it wishes. How true this is today. Despite this you can summon up a more flexible approach – that is if you really wish to do so. In all probability you will be quite content to show the more intransigent side of your nature until bedtime. Make sure this doesn't put you on someone's really bad side.

21 TUESDAY *Moon Age Day 24 Moon Sign Capricorn*

The lunar high comes as something of a surprise this week and you could quite suddenly find yourself catapulted into the spotlight, perhaps in a number of different ways. You should find others being particularly helpful and can rely on the fact that your present level of good luck is likely to be significantly higher than usual.

22 WEDNESDAY *Moon Age Day 25 Moon Sign Capricorn*

This is your time and you don't have to defer to others, simply because they seem to know more about situations than you do. Your influence is strong and getting the better of people who have used you in the past is something you should relish. However, you won't do this with any venom because that simply isn't your way.

23 THURSDAY *Moon Age Day 26 Moon Sign Capricorn*

You should find most areas of life something of a joy today. The hangover from the lunar high, together with other positive planetary trends, conspires to bring you a feeling of success. What probably matters the most at the moment is the fact that you realise how strong your popularity is and can therefore make the most of it.

24 FRIDAY *Moon Age Day 27 Moon Sign Aquarius*

You should now be happier to take on a more freewheeling approach to life. True this isn't the Capricorn way as a rule but you simply can't help the feeling that natural changes must come along. It takes courage to follow such trends through to their logical conclusion but Capricorn has plenty of guts, even if it is sometimes a little reserved.

25 SATURDAY *Moon Age Day 28 Moon Sign Aquarius*

Personal relationships should feel more stable now and offer you the chance to retreat a little from the practical aspects of your life and into the bosom of your family. When you are dealing with the world at large it would be sensible not to advertise your own perceived limitations to others or you could just end up highlighting them unnecessarily.

26 SUNDAY *Moon Age Day 29 Moon Sign Pisces*

A matter close to your heart takes up a good amount of your time and might slow down your success rate in a number of other situations. It is possible that you are worrying unnecessarily and it might be an idea to seek out the help and support of a family member or perhaps a really good friend.

27 MONDAY *Moon Age Day 0 Moon Sign Pisces*

There should be plenty to smile about at present, especially when it comes to family matters. Even in relationships with those you don't know well you should discover points of contact that bring warmth to these associations. You are able to understand what friends are asking of you, even when they are virtually silent.

28 TUESDAY *Moon Age Day 1 Moon Sign Aries*

Your domestic partner may prove to you just how much they care by making a general fuss of you today. Although you will appreciate their efforts, you are turning your mind more to the outside world and less to your home. If you think about it, though, there will be ways in which you can mix business and pleasure.

29 WEDNESDAY *Moon Age Day 2 Moon Sign Aries*

You might only be looking for average progress today and might feel that there are those about who seem to have a vested interest in preventing you from getting ahead. In reality this is almost certainly not the case but if it is possible for you to get hold of the wrong end of the stick you are likely to do so under present trends.

30 THURSDAY *Moon Age Day 3 Moon Sign Taurus*

Where new possibilities are concerned you are presently looking beyond simple curiosity and towards the most practical way to apply yourself to them. Give yourself a pat on the back for recent successes but avoid any tendency to complacency. Trends also indicate that this ought to be a fairly comfortable time materially.

31 FRIDAY *Moon Age Day 4 Moon Sign Taurus*

It now occurs to you that you are in a good position to streamline your life in some way. Use today to make changes, especially ones that involve getting rid of some of the deadwood that is accumulating in your life. Some Capricorns will now feel a greater than usual desire to travel, and if this is the case for you, perhaps make some plans for the weekend.

April
2017

1 SATURDAY *Moon Age Day 5 Moon Sign Gemini*

You will enjoy being the centre of attention wherever you go today. It would be a shame if the favourable planetary aspects creating this tendency were wasted, simply because this was nothing more than a routine day. Put yourself out to make sure there are social possibilities this Saturday.

2 SUNDAY *Moon Age Day 6 Moon Sign Gemini*

A financial issue is apt to prove somewhat complicated, leading you to seek the advice of someone who is more in the know than you are. Don't avoid discussions, simply because you are not in a chatty frame of mind. Things need sorting out and you won't manage that without talking.

3 MONDAY *Moon Age Day 7 Moon Sign Cancer*

Some setbacks appear to be unavoidable today. The lunar low makes you less able to push through obstacles and as a result leave you feeling stuck. The best way to deal with this sort of situation is to tell yourself that in a couple of days your usual flexible mood will begin to return and that in the meantime you can do some planning.

4 TUESDAY *Moon Age Day 8 Moon Sign Cancer*

The lunar low still prevents you from pushing forward with any real dynamism and it seems likely that you will find major plans foundering if you push too hard. Everyone needs to recharge their batteries from time to time and it appears that this is what you are about for the moment. By tomorrow things should be much improved.

5 WEDNESDAY *Moon Age Day 9 Moon Sign Leo*

A professional issue could cause a rather tense atmosphere today – that is unless you take it by the scruff of the neck and sort it out immediately. You need to be very direct in all your dealings right now because hedging your bets just doesn't work under present trends. Friends might also display a lack of confidence in you, which could be disquieting.

6 THURSDAY *Moon Age Day 10 Moon Sign Leo*

Practical issues and general run-of-the-mill situations are likely to take up much of your time today. Although you are likely to get plenty done, this probably could not be considered a particularly successful day. Happily, you creative potential is especially good now so try to capitalise on this in some way.

7 FRIDAY *Moon Age Day 11 Moon Sign Leo*

You know the value of self-reliance and are not afraid to go your own way. This is particularly true today. Your attitude is rock solid, causing others to have a deep and abiding confidence in your decisions. The fact that this appears to place an extra burden on you is something you don't recognise at all.

8 SATURDAY *Moon Age Day 12 Moon Sign Virgo*

You are likely to be happiest when amongst those you love this weekend, particularly today. It isn't that you feel threatened by the outside world but you are very domestically minded right now. Your home is your castle and for the moment, you want to keep the drawbridge up. This should make for a comfortable and enjoyable day.

9 SUNDAY *Moon Age Day 13 Moon Sign Virgo*

Coming to terms with a personal issue is part of what today is about. Be confident in your dealings with others and avoid giving anyone the impression that you are not certain regarding decisions you wish to take. Friends should prove to be especially helpful at the moment and genuinely do want to lend a hand.

10 MONDAY ☿ *Moon Age Day 14 Moon Sign Libra*

Today you should take professional issues in your stride, proving once again how reliable you are, even when under some small stress. You can't expect everyone to agree with your point of view at the moment but in the end you will invariably turn out to be right. People should listen to Capricorn more than they do.

11 TUESDAY ☿ *Moon Age Day 15 Moon Sign Libra*

Some minor mishaps are possible today, although luckily you should be able to view them in a humorous way. It is hard to take anything particularly seriously now and you really want to have fun. The practical joker within you really comes to the fore, and this trait is likely to continue for a little while.

12 WEDNESDAY ☿ *Moon Age Day 16 Moon Sign Scorpio*

During the midweek there is a very strong emphasis on the fun side of life and it is possible that you find it difficult to take certain matters seriously. You might have to pretend that you do, though only for the sake of those around you. Don't be afraid to give yourself a pat on the back for a recent success that is likely to lead to others.

13 THURSDAY ☿ *Moon Age Day 17 Moon Sign Scorpio*

This is another good day to be around the people you care for the most. Although you have been a distinctly social person on quite a few occasions this month, in the main you are happiest when you understand your surroundings and the people within it. Still, one or two friends may prove to be positively inspirational.

14 FRIDAY ☿ *Moon Age Day 18 Moon Sign Scorpio*

Having fun is likely to be your number one priority this Friday. Although this is somewhat difficult in the midst of a busy life, you do presently have the ability to mix business with pleasure and to enjoy them both. Seek out people who haven't been around recently and take the chance to have a chat with them.

15 SATURDAY ☿ *Moon Age Day 19 Moon Sign Sagittarius*

It is towards the practical aspects of life that your mind now turns. You can discover a number of new ways to get ahead outside of work and should also be enjoying the cut and thrust of an active life that could involve new friends. Family matters might have to be left on the backburner for a short while.

16 SUNDAY ☿ *Moon Age Day 20 Moon Sign Sagittarius*

Get ready to take a starring role in life this week. Planetary trends are lining up once again to offer you a great deal of incentive. Although your practical progress could be marred because this is Sunday, you will have no difficulty whatsoever in making valuable allies. New friendships are also likely to be formed at this time.

17 MONDAY ☿ *Moon Age Day 21 Moon Sign Capricorn*

Almost anything you have planned for today should go well, as much as anything because of the level of effort you are willing and able to put in. Today's planetary trends bring a strong element of luck to bear on most of what you do, making this definitely a time to back your hunches all the way.

18 TUESDAY ☿ *Moon Age Day 22 Moon Sign Capricorn*

There are now great opportunities for gain and ones that you will not want to pass by. Shopping today could lead to the discovery of genuine bargains, while the social possibilities also look particularly good. If there isn't much happening around you, the chances are that it's you who is not trying hard enough.

19 WEDNESDAY ☿ *Moon Age Day 23 Moon Sign Capricorn*

If you are required to negotiate between warring factions amongst family and friends you should rise to the challenge readily, whilst at the same time showing that you definitely have your practical head on at present. Smoothing over disagreements is easy for you today, not least of all because Capricorn is a natural peacemaker in any case.

20 THURSDAY ☿ *Moon Age Day 24 Moon Sign Aquarius*

Better by far today to take life steadily and to make certain that you have your facts right, no matter what you undertake. Routines are not difficult to deal with at this stage though not everyone will be quite as helpful as you might have hoped, especially when it comes to your work. It would be sensible to check most details now.

21 FRIDAY ☿ *Moon Age Day 25 Moon Sign Aquarius*

You may find that others expect you to back down over a certain issue today and that's something that is difficult for the average Capricorn to do. However, it has to be said that a little flexibility at this stage could see you reaping greater benefits further down the line. When it comes to speaking words of love you won't have any problem today.

22 SATURDAY ☿ *Moon Age Day 26 Moon Sign Pisces*

Getting on with what is necessary might be something of a chore and it is quite possible that you will decide to alter your routines to find a little inspiration. Not everyone finds this easy to come to terms with but those you really care about will co-operate. Getting others to follow your lead is far from difficult under present astrological trends.

23 SUNDAY ☿ *Moon Age Day 27 Moon Sign Pisces*

This would be a very good day for collecting and collating any sort of information, some of which proves to be very important later. You will be more than ready to move ahead quickly with important matters and keen to get involved in situations you could well have shied away from previously.

24 MONDAY ☿ *Moon Age Day 28 Moon Sign Pisces*

A professional boost could so easily come along at the beginning of this week. The help and support of colleagues could prove to be extremely important and it seems that you could benefit from some extra help from directions that you hadn't expected. Close personal contacts might have some news to impart.

25 TUESDAY ☿ *Moon Age Day 0 Moon Sign Aries*

Your constant desire to keep life on an even keel could be somewhat upset by the foolish actions of others. Ignore this if you can and opt instead for a positive day, with plenty of social contact and a continue determination to break through barriers. Stay away from negative people who only have doom and gloom to impart.

26 WEDNESDAY ☿ *Moon Age Day 1 Moon Sign Aries*

It isn't hard for you to get on with anyone right now and you will have a particular fondness for those who can be termed 'real characters'. Such individuals bring out the slightly quirky side of your own nature and stop you from being too serious about anything. What you most want from today is a laugh.

27 THURSDAY ☿ *Moon Age Day 2 Moon Sign Taurus*

Approaching life with the sort of abandon that is sometimes missing from the Capricorn life, you are now entertaining to have around. Of course there is the chance that you will say something that will cause you embarrassment later – but what does that matter? The Goat is in full swing and everyone wants to listen.

28 FRIDAY ☿ *Moon Age Day 3 Moon Sign Taurus*

Today you should have the ability to get up and make good things happen for yourself and take complete charge of most situations. If you come across anything that is genuinely out of your control you will need to rely on trust, even if this is sometimes difficult for you. Capricorn invariably wants to run the entire show – but this just isn't always possible.

29 SATURDAY ☿ *Moon Age Day 4 Moon Sign Gemini*

Your levels of concentration are probably not all they should be at the moment. If you know that this is the case then right from the start you need to ask someone to remind you of particular jobs you have to do. Relying on others is not presently to your liking, though you could find you make new friends as a result. Learn a little trust today.

30 SUNDAY ☿ *Moon Age Day 5 Moon Sign Gemini*

Don't wait to be asked today – take what you want from life and deal with the consequences later. It's highly unlikely that you would make any enemies on the way because you are so charming right now. The positive trends spurred on by present planetary positions remain around for some time and you may as well make use of them.

May

2017

1 MONDAY ☿ *Moon Age Day 6 Moon Sign Cancer*

The lunar low is almost certain to slow things down, though not disproportionately. All you really notice this month is the fact that things are not going exactly your way. If you stay away from material considerations and concentrate on having fun, the position of the Moon won't affect you at all.

2 TUESDAY ☿ *Moon Age Day 7 Moon Sign Cancer*

There are some tests of your patience to be dealt with today, but the same rules as yesterday still apply. Family matters are easy to deal with but you could find a certain restless streak beginning to develop within you. Go for anything that feels different but do stay away from taking undue risks for the moment.

3 WEDNESDAY ☿ *Moon Age Day 8 Moon Sign Leo*

You are now in a very good position to call the shots where future plans are concerned. What matters is that you are doing your homework, which others may not manage so well. This means your point of view is reasoned and difficult to fault. In business, you tend to be extremely shrewd at present.

4 THURSDAY *Moon Age Day 9 Moon Sign Leo*

You should find yourself more attracted by casual friendships now than intense relationships. Your present matter-of-fact attitude does not wish to be stifled by too much heartache so practical matters are closer to your heart right now. Don't be surprised if you find yourself taking a sudden and rather unexpected change in direction.

5 FRIDAY *Moon Age Day 10 Moon Sign Virgo*

A good deal of what happens now depends on the say so of others. This is slightly frustrating because you may get a good deal of the way down a road of your own construction only to find that you need some sort of permission to proceed. Try to remain patient and argue your case eloquently.

6 SATURDAY *Moon Age Day 11 Moon Sign Virgo*

Your ability to command attention and impress others can be put to the test today. With plenty going for you in a general sense and material situations still looking good, it's time to go for gold. Although not everyone appears to have your best interests at heart, when it matters most friends come up trumps.

7 SUNDAY *Moon Age Day 12 Moon Sign Libra*

Family matters should now be putting a smile on your face. Younger relatives especially have the ability to make you laugh but so do many other people and situations because your sense of humour is so highly charged now. Plan for a different sort of Sunday, with the possibility of movement and travel.

8 MONDAY *Moon Age Day 13 Moon Sign Libra*

The more widespread and different the company you find yourself in today, the better you are likely to feel. Abandoning for the moment thoughts of security and comfort, you may be seeking to put yourself to the test in a physical sense. Remember birthdays in the family and amongst your friends. This is a good emailing day.

9 TUESDAY *Moon Age Day 14 Moon Sign Libra*

Your mind could turn towards creative pursuits of one sort or another. Yours is a very practical zodiac sign, so anything arty tends to have an everyday function for you too. Since you are an Earth sign, perhaps you might turn to something like pottery? There could also be some movement on the romantic front.

10 WEDNESDAY *Moon Age Day 15 Moon Sign Scorpio*

It would be best to keep your feelings out in the open today. Your zodiac sign has a tendency to bottle things up on occasion, which is very rarely the right way to proceed. You could experience some small difficulty with mechanical gadgets of one sort or another and might have to enlist some help.

11 THURSDAY *Moon Age Day 16 Moon Sign Scorpio*

Today is definitely one of those times during which you get out of life almost exactly what you put into it. If you want to be lethargic, situations won't demand much of you but you won't make the gains either. Better by far to go for gold and then to glory in the attention that comes your way.

12 FRIDAY *Moon Age Day 17 Moon Sign Sagittarius*

Today is apt to find you in a high-spirited mood and ready for fun at present. This attitude is infectious, as you are about to find out. Your popularity remains high and might even increase. All the attention coming your way at the moment is great, but it isn't what Capricorn usually looks for or expects.

13 SATURDAY *Moon Age Day 18 Moon Sign Sagittarius*

Matters at work should be quite fulfilling, even though so many of you won't actually be working on a Saturday. What you can do is to plan for later, though don't devote the whole day to this area of life. People around you clearly wish to have fun and with the way you are feeling at present, you will want to join in.

14 SUNDAY *Moon Age Day 19 Moon Sign Sagittarius*

Today should be fairly enjoyable but some of the glitter might be taken off social situations if the odd wet blanket comes along. Although there isn't really a great deal you can do to avoid such an eventuality, you should be able to cheer up even the most depressing of people with your present bubbly nature.

15 MONDAY *Moon Age Day 20 Moon Sign Capricorn*

Call in a few favours today because it is quite obvious that almost everyone is on your side. This is a time to remember, or at least it will be if you only put in a modicum of effort. General good fortune aids almost any enterprise you choose right now and relationships should be the cause of much happiness.

16 TUESDAY *Moon Age Day 21 Moon Sign Capricorn*

This is the time to put fresh ideas to the test. You won't want to feel in any way fettered and have a strong determination to do what pleases you. Since you are presently so charming, it is unlikely that anyone would deliberately stand in your way. Don't be afraid of some limited and very well thought out speculation.

17 WEDNESDAY *Moon Age Day 22 Moon Sign Aquarius*

A bustling and active period comes along and you probably won't have any time to spare at all right now. That's fine because as a Capricorn you never mind being busy but it could mean that someone is not getting quite the level of attention they rightfully deserve. Just do your best and be aware that you need to keep in touch with many people in your environment.

18 THURSDAY *Moon Age Day 23 Moon Sign Aquarius*

If you can't immediately get your own way in family discussions, you could turn a little awkward and reveal an overbearing streak. In your view, this is all because others are not being reasonable in their attitude – but they might think the same about you. A degree of sincere compromise is called for at this time.

19 FRIDAY *Moon Age Day 24 Moon Sign Pisces*

Romantic and social developments are looking good around now. With the Sun still just in your solar fifth house you are able to show your affection even more than is sometimes the case and you have it within you to make a real fuss of your partner or lover. Make sure you pack some fun into this Friday.

20 SATURDAY *Moon Age Day 25 Moon Sign Pisces*

The possibilities for personal and romantic attachments are now especially good. Make use of this period ahead of a busy new working week to show someone just how much you really care. The response you get at present is likely to be extremely good and you should have too much difficulty with even the prickliest characters.

21 SUNDAY *Moon Age Day 26 Moon Sign Pisces*

What an excellent period this would be for coming up with new ideas. Multi-tasking is your bag and you can easily handle several different matters at once. You should also be more than willing to take on challenges that, in the past, would have worried you. Stand by a family member who really seems to need your support at the moment.

22 MONDAY *Moon Age Day 27 Moon Sign Aries*

Today's trends suggest that you will be in the market for spoiling yourself and for having fun. A difficult situation from the past can be turned around quickly and you seem to have all that it takes to get things moving very positively in a business sense, too. This appears to be an excellent planetary spell for most Capricorns.

23 TUESDAY *Moon Age Day 28 Moon Sign Aries*

Some Capricorn quick-thinking could now prove to be particularly important today. Not all the planetary positions are equally helpful now but you won't let this stop you from making the sort of progress that is so useful to you. Avoid putting energy into pointless tasks and settle instead for a slightly less hectic regime. Take some time out to consider family members.

24 WEDNESDAY *Moon Age Day 29 Moon Sign Taurus*

The best course of action today would involve spending time with both loved ones and friends; certainly the sort of people who take pleasure in supporting you. Though you have plenty of energy at present and should be willing to be on the go most of the time, it is important not to scatter your energies too liberally.

25 THURSDAY *Moon Age Day 0 Moon Sign Taurus*

You could be suffering from a little disorganisation. In all probability this fact won't matter too much because you are presently so good at convincing others to do things on your behalf. Make the most of friendships; these have a great deal to offer you at the moment, whilst romantic urges are not quite so strong.

26 FRIDAY *Moon Age Day 1 Moon Sign Gemini*

You should avoid unnecessary distractions today in your efforts to get on in life generally. It is very important that you do not lose sight of your most important priorities and that you keep up your efforts to get ahead in a general sense. Socially speaking you should be active and very entertaining.

27 SATURDAY *Moon Age Day 2 Moon Sign Gemini*

Once you have made up your mind to a particular course of action this Saturday, you need to follow it through. Friends and relatives alike should line up to offer whatever help they can at this important time. Trends have moved on and now the most important sphere of life is deep, personal relationships. Capricorn is in the market for love!

28 SUNDAY *Moon Age Day 3 Moon Sign Cancer*

Make a conscious choice to slow life down today and avoid taking on things that you know from the very start are going to be awkward. Give yourself time to think and to reach conclusions that are based on a mixture of intuition and commonsense. Be aware that you may not be too lucky with money today.

29 MONDAY *Moon Age Day 4 Moon Sign Cancer*

There may be deeper and more emotional matters that require your attention today. Initially it could seem that this will spoil your fun, though this really isn't likely to turn out to be the case. Mixing business with pleasure is also possible later in the day, when it should become obvious that the lunar low is moving away.

30 TUESDAY *Moon Age Day 5 Moon Sign Leo*

This is an especially good time to enjoy music or art and to make the sort of impression that won't be forgotten by those around you. The cultured side of your zodiac sign is really beginning to show and you might also discover one or two talents that you have been hiding so well, even you didn't know you had them!

31 WEDNESDAY *Moon Age Day 6 Moon Sign Leo*

If you can't get the emotional support you feel you need and deserve from others, you could feel somewhat alone today. Of course this isn't quite the issue with you that it would be with some zodiac signs but it is good to know that you have people on your side. Spend a little time talking sensibly to relatives and close friends.

June

2017

1 THURSDAY *Moon Age Day 7 Moon Sign Virgo*

Look out for a few ups and downs in finances at this time. You may need to adapt more positively to outside circumstances and also possibly recognise a few limitations that are likely to be placed upon you now. In terms of personal relationships the present period should prove to be secure and can promote greater affection generally.

2 FRIDAY *Moon Age Day 8 Moon Sign Virgo*

This is a day for enjoying the social whirl and for communicating your ideas to others. You may need a bit more mental focus because you are still not seeing all situations the way they really are. However, your confidence in your own abilities is on the increase and you might take a few little chances today you wouldn't have considered yesterday.

3 SATURDAY *Moon Age Day 9 Moon Sign Virgo*

You won't have to try very hard to impress anyone at the moment. However, compromise is a word you do need to keep in mind and there will be no gain at all now from refusing to adapt, especially if your heart tells you this is the thing to do. All the same, impulsive actions are still less likely to bring rewards.

4 SUNDAY *Moon Age Day 10 Moon Sign Libra*

You can gain both emotionally and perhaps financially from the actions of loved ones. Your mood is warm and sensitive at present and you can be moved quite easily, perhaps by a memory, a piece of music or something that you read. In this frame of mind, you may decide to look up people you haven't seen for a while.

5 MONDAY *Moon Age Day 11 Moon Sign Libra*

Long-term plans and the strategies necessary to get what you want from your working life are at the centre of your focus at the start of another week. Don't be too quick to jump to conclusions where the apparent actions of others are concerned. Give situations time to mature and you may be surprised by the eventual outcome.

6 TUESDAY *Moon Age Day 12 Moon Sign Scorpio*

A boost comes along as far as your social life is concerned. Taken together with other positives in your life you can make this interesting time, once the concerns of the material world have been dealt with. You could also notice an upturn in general fortune and financial strength beginning at any time now.

7 WEDNESDAY *Moon Age Day 13 Moon Sign Scorpio*

Your partner could now play a more dominant role in your life but only because that is the way you want the situation to be. In other areas of life, you would be well advised to look very carefully at suggestions that are being made which somehow have a bearing on your working circumstances. Perhaps some negotiation is necessary?

8 THURSDAY *Moon Age Day 14 Moon Sign Sagittarius*

This period of the working week coincides with trends that particularly favour co-operative ventures of any sort. Be willing to put yourself out for the sake of the group as a whole, whilst continuing to plough your own furrow in other ways. What you shouldn't do today is to put yourself completely out on a limb.

9 FRIDAY *Moon Age Day 15 Moon Sign Sagittarius*

You want to be in charge of finances now, even though others may not agree that this is a good idea. What you must do is to put forward a reasoned argument, explaining your point of view. If that doesn't work, leave things alone for a day or two. You should also leave time today to talk about less serious matters and to have fun.

10 SATURDAY *Moon Age Day 16 Moon Sign Sagittarius*

It is likely that the things people say today boost your ego and make you generally more confident. It may not have been a crackerjack of a week for some but there are better things in store. Capricorn may well undergo a phase of mental realignment today and so you could find yourself rather less physically active.

11 SUNDAY *Moon Age Day 17 Moon Sign Capricorn*

The lunar high this month has some very practical applications, which suit you down to the ground. Your sphere of influence is strong, both at work and at home. Changes you have wanted to implement for some time now become entirely possible, and the more so if you show yourself to be dynamic.

12 MONDAY *Moon Age Day 18 Moon Sign Capricorn*

This is a bonus period for personal relationships and for love especially. It isn't at all difficult to show your partner or sweetheart how you feel about them. Since the lunar high invariably brings better than average luck, it is also fair to suggest that you can chance your arm in some way today.

13 TUESDAY *Moon Age Day 19 Moon Sign Aquarius*

Things that happen today could enhance your career prospects no end. You need to keep your eyes open because there are some helpful people and situations around. If you are presently engaged on a health kick of some sort, just remember that success comes through methodical application and there is no quick fix.

14 WEDNESDAY *Moon Age Day 20 Moon Sign Aquarius*

Trends provide some incentives during this midweek period and help you to latch on to any practical advantage that is around at the moment. Your confidence continues to grow, though the later part of this week could bring some small reversals. In a general sense your life is moving forward, even though the process is steady at present.

15 THURSDAY *Moon Age Day 21 Moon Sign Aquarius*

The desire for personal freedom feels particularly strong around now, perhaps leading to you breaking out of some situations that no longer suit you. Not everyone is going to understand your reasoning, though you do have a particularly good ability to explain yourself at the moment.

16 FRIDAY *Moon Age Day 22 Moon Sign Pisces*

You easily express charm, grace and harmony at the moment, so there is no wonder that you are wowing almost everyone you come across. This would be a good time to concentrate on love and also to make a startling impression on people who can have an important part to play in your life in the months to come.

17 SATURDAY *Moon Age Day 23 Moon Sign Pisces*

With the Sun now in your solar seventh house, personal relationships tend to be under the spotlight. This is still a fine time for romance but you will be redrawing certain rules in less intimate contacts. It is entirely possible that new friends will come into your life around now, not a common event for Capricorn.

18 SUNDAY *Moon Age Day 24 Moon Sign Aries*

You will almost certainly have good ideas now for improving work-based situations, even though Sunday might be a day of rest as far as you are concerned. In between finding excellent ways to enjoy yourself, it is clear that you are casting your mind into the future and coming up with some cracking schemes.

19 MONDAY *Moon Age Day 25 Moon Sign Aries*

Look out for some new ideas that should be coming along at any time now. You know what you want from life today and in general it shouldn't be difficult to get it. Showing concern for those in trouble is pretty much what you are about as a person and this really does show across the coming days.

20 TUESDAY *Moon Age Day 26 Moon Sign Taurus*

If you want assistance for personal efforts, you will have the necessary cheek to ask for it today. Few aspects of life are working against your best interests right now and in some ways you find this to be an important turning point generally. Although changes look like being low-key, they may turn out to be very significant in the end.

21 WEDNESDAY *Moon Age Day 27 Moon Sign Taurus*

Look out for some hopeful news arriving regarding situations that might not appear to have been working out well for you recently. There is plenty of room for romance in your life at present and it appears that you are taking the time to show your partner or someone you really like how very kind you can be.

22 THURSDAY *Moon Age Day 28 Moon Sign Gemini*

All involvement with family members should be a joy at present. Offers of travel may not seem quite so appealing as they could have done a few days ago and you might be feeling quite happy to stay in one place, as long as the company is stimulating. Romance is certainly to the forefront of many Capricorn minds today.

23 FRIDAY *Moon Age Day 29 Moon Sign Gemini*

Relationships may offer the best way forward at the present time, as would a shopping excursion or perhaps a social event of some sort. Being with friends should be the most stimulating activity, though you have it within you to mix business with pleasure at the moment and can easily make profit from what seems a purely personal event.

24 SATURDAY *Moon Age Day 0 Moon Sign Cancer*

If things are developing nicely in any area of your life, avoid taking any risks with them now. The lunar low could bring some negative influences to bear over the advantages you have built for yourself in the last week or two, so you should exercise extra care today. Emotionally speaking, you are likely to feel stronger and generally more resilient.

25 SUNDAY *Moon Age Day 1 Moon Sign Cancer*

The lunar low is still present but there are also progressive trends in your chart, especially those dealing with social matters and ways of having fun. You might be slightly restricted in a material sense but that won't prevent you from finding enjoyment. However, you will probably feel more comfortable within your family.

26 MONDAY *Moon Age Day 2 Moon Sign Leo*

You could be feeling touchy and somewhat reluctant to join in with a crowd today. The little things that some people do will be rather annoying, though in reality the problem probably lies with your own point of view. To alleviate these tendencies, talk to those you live with and avoid meeting new people just now.

27 TUESDAY *Moon Age Day 3 Moon Sign Leo*

You ought to find yourself in amongst just the right company today and can make the most positive of impressions when it counts. Your social and love life is likely to by far your most fulfilling part of life around now and you won't have any problem at all getting others to join in the fun you are instigating.

28 WEDNESDAY *Moon Age Day 4 Moon Sign Leo*

The ability to get along well and easily with others is now very strong indeed. Although you may not be letting your hair down big-time and will still be exercising some caution, you have powerful social inclinations now and want to share your opinions with others. A short journey might suit you well.

29 THURSDAY *Moon Age Day 5 Moon Sign Virgo*

Romantic and social activity tends to be happy and harmonious around this time. There could be one or two surprises in the offing, plus the possibility of getting something that you have wanted for quite some time. It will be necessary to see one or two jobs through to completion if you really want to profit now.

30 FRIDAY *Moon Age Day 6 Moon Sign Virgo*

Things are likely to be rather hectic today and there won't be too much time to catch your breath. To a great extent you have to rely on your intuition and upon the advice of people who you know to have your best interests at heart. Look out for very rewarding situations at work, mainly because of the effort you put in.

July

2017 

1 SATURDAY *Moon Age Day 7 Moon Sign Libra*

This could be a good day for family get-togethers or reunions of some sort. With a slightly nostalgic streak taking over, perhaps you are looking on the internet, to see if you can locate some of those buddies you haven't seen for years. If you find them, be prepared for one or two surprises.

2 SUNDAY *Moon Age Day 8 Moon Sign Libra*

This is another of those periods during which you are happy to be in the social spotlight. Capricorn is far more gregarious at the moment than would usually be the case. Don't panic, however, because you still maintain the slight inner reserve that marks you out as different from the showier zodiac signs.

3 MONDAY *Moon Age Day 9 Moon Sign Scorpio*

Trends assist you to bend situations in your career your own way and you also stand a chance of making a good impression on others at the moment. Your confidence is certainly not lacking, though you could also discover that someone you counted as a friend is not doing you any favours. All the same, don't over-react.

4 TUESDAY *Moon Age Day 10 Moon Sign Scorpio*

Today could see you feeling emotionally tense, maybe as a result of the behaviour of colleagues. Although you demonstrate great loyalty to those around you this month, it won't always be coming back to you in the way you would wish or expect. Some situations need a definite dose of common sense and intuition.

5 WEDNESDAY *Moon Age Day 11 Moon Sign Scorpio*

The more ambitious you are today, the better you are likely to be getting on. Keep your ears open because even the most casual of conversations could be carrying some surprising but useful news. In any situation, it can be quite crucial to strike while the iron is not. At work, you are a force to be reckoned with.

6 THURSDAY *Moon Age Day 12 Moon Sign Sagittarius*

Now a fairly cautious approach is required where money and financial affairs in general is concerned, but the same cannot be said in the realm of romance. Here, Capricorn is the king or queen. Without thinking, you heap so many compliments on the object of your desire that they will be putty in your hands.

7 FRIDAY *Moon Age Day 13 Moon Sign Sagittarius*

Your social life continues to be a main focus of life. There are trends around at the moment that would make this period ideal for travel, so maybe a holiday is on the cards? Avoid allowing any of your plans to be too much altered by the attitude and opinions of people who are not really involved in them at all.

8 SATURDAY *Moon Age Day 14 Moon Sign Capricorn*

It's time to push ahead with your dreams and schemes because if you are going to make anything of them, this is the most likely period. Capricorn is especially unsettled today, though not in a negative sense. All through the month, travel has been a distinct possibility and that eventuality is even more likely now.

9 SUNDAY *Moon Age Day 15 Moon Sign Capricorn*

Most everyday issues go according to plan and progress should be generally smooth. You can negotiate potential difficulties without really recognising they are present and should also enjoy a high degree of popularity in a general sense. Best of all, general good luck is likely to pay you a visit.

10 MONDAY *Moon Age Day 16 Moon Sign Capricorn*

Some of the problems you come across today simply cannot be overcome using pure logic. This is the usual first resort of Capricorn, but you can be quite intuitive too, particularly at the moment. Take a sideways look at situations and avoid taking the most obvious approach if it feels wrong.

11 TUESDAY *Moon Age Day 17 Moon Sign Aquarius*

Keep your eyes and ears open today. Almost any information can be of use to you and although you don't generally deal in gossip or chit-chat, you may well be more inclined to do so right now. This is a Tuesday that should find you busy, even when there is nothing much to do.

12 WEDNESDAY *Moon Age Day 18 Moon Sign Aquarius*

You are in a very good position to influence others. This applies particularly at work. Even if a degree of gentle coercion is necessary, as long as you know the end genuinely does justify the means, you should go ahead. Once work is out of the way, you might be especially pleased to be out of doors.

13 THURSDAY *Moon Age Day 19 Moon Sign Pisces*

The most casual of meetings could turn into something much more interesting today. Although there are one or two people around now who may not be trustworthy, seeing through such individuals isn't at all difficult. The most appealing thing about today is the sheer volume of work you can get through.

14 FRIDAY *Moon Age Day 20 Moon Sign Pisces*

You have a real thirst for fresh experiences now. Seeking out change and variety in your life is likely to be extremely important and there are very few difficult trends to deal with right now. Although you are still good at problem solving, it is possible that you might have to seek out an expert during today or tomorrow.

15 SATURDAY *Moon Age Day 21 Moon Sign Aries*

What really does matter today is the number and quality of contacts you are making. It is for this reason that you can't really afford to put your feet up too much. Action is the key to success, no matter what sphere of life you are looking at. A strong attachment could be formed as the weekend moves on.

16 SUNDAY *Moon Age Day 22 Moon Sign Aries*

You might find yourself compelled to go over the ins and outs of an emotional matter today, something that you would often prefer to avoid altogether if you could. Don't be too quick to judge either the motives or actions of another person, just in case you find yourself facing the same situation some day.

17 MONDAY *Moon Age Day 23 Moon Sign Aries*

Trends bring you increased concentration and perception, which lifts the possibilities for the start of the working week no end. Although you can now get on very well in a practical sense, it is the social trends that count the most. A very unusual streak comes along and the Goat is now far more willing to look at long shots and calculated risks.

18 TUESDAY *Moon Age Day 24 Moon Sign Taurus*

Today you should be in a good position to call the shots, not least of all because those closest to you, especially at work, are more than happy to follow your lead. There are potential gains to be made in a number of different areas of life at present, and work might be the number one area. Focus your attention and strive to do your best.

19 WEDNESDAY *Moon Age Day 25 Moon Sign Taurus*

Less outgoing than you have been for a few days, you will probably find that spending some time on your own now has great appeal. All the same you won't be losing your desire to find adventure, though for the moment at least some of this could come from the pages of a particularly good book or from an appealing movie.

20 THURSDAY *Moon Age Day 26 Moon Sign Gemini*

You might be in for one or two slightly unpleasant experiences if you put your trust in the wrong sort of people right now. Use your intuition and your Capricorn, Earth-sign common sense when assessing anything. If you are involved in any sort of sporting activity, now is the time to go for gold and to win!

21 FRIDAY *Moon Age Day 27 Moon Sign Gemini*

An even greater interest in what makes the world tick can set this Friday apart, though quite a few Capricorns will find themselves to be in relaxation mode. There are some obstacles in the weekend ahead and directly conflicting interests to be dealt with. Prepare for this by resting when you can and enjoying some careful thought.

22 SATURDAY *Moon Age Day 28 Moon Sign Cancer*

While the lunar low is around it might be sensible to allow your partner or another family member to deal with some of the major issues on the home front. Although you can hold your own if you are at work, be prepared for the fact that there may not be the same feeling of progress that has been around for quite a few days now.

23 SUNDAY *Moon Age Day 0 Moon Sign Cancer*

Take things steadily today because there is a possibility that your life is beset with small pressures and issues that just won't work out the way you want. There is absolutely no point in becoming frustrated with the situation. In any case, by tomorrow everything should be on a more even keel.

24 MONDAY *Moon Age Day 1 Moon Sign Leo*

Your social life and relationships are now under the spotlight and might be found wanting in some way. Certainly you are likely to make far-reaching changes, either now or soon and it is likely that these will leave you with more time to enjoy the company of people you like a great deal.

25 TUESDAY *Moon Age Day 2 Moon Sign Leo*

Things go much better in pairs today and this is the case whether the topic is business or romance. Although you are quite capable of managing on your own, the stronger social trends brought about by the position of the inner planets at present should not be ignored. Friends are likely to demand most of your attention later in the day.

26 WEDNESDAY *Moon Age Day 3 Moon Sign Virgo*

You are now caught up in a swiftly-moving period with aspects of your life changing quite rapidly. Don't be fooled into thinking that someone you might mix with professionally knows better than you do how to run your life. The fact is that only you have the most intimate understanding of the way things truly are.

27 THURSDAY *Moon Age Day 4 Moon Sign Virgo*

A spirit of harmony and co-operation prevails and even increases at the moment. It is clear that your partner or family members have your best interests at heart and you are now far more willing to share the essence of your nature. The closed book that Capricorn can sometimes be is now open to view, at least by some.

28 FRIDAY *Moon Age Day 5 Moon Sign Libra*

Though you are clearly thinking big and maybe acting quite big too, deep inside you are not nearly as sure of yourself as you might pretend. It's time to admit a few of your faults, though of course not to everyone. Someone you consider either older or wiser than you are would be more than pleased to listen to what you have to say.

29 SATURDAY *Moon Age Day 6 Moon Sign Libra*

There should be much happening in personal relationships that will make you feel quite joyful. You could do worse than to get intimate with someone you really care about and there probably hasn't been a better time this year for Capricorn when it comes to new love blossoming and growing apace.

30 SUNDAY *Moon Age Day 7 Moon Sign Libra*

The idea of getting out of doors seems really appealing to you at present, and the warmth of the summer breezes also encourages you to look beyond your own immediate vicinity for new experiences. Any change you make at the moment will do you good but you might have to settle one or two issues at home first.

31 MONDAY *Moon Age Day 8 Moon Sign Scorpio*

When it comes to money matters, you should find that present planetary influences will be very much more than neutral. That doesn't mean you will be spending lavishly because in the main the things you enjoy at the moment are not likely to cost you a penny. Today could mark a period based around friendship.

August

2017

1 TUESDAY *Moon Age Day 9 Moon Sign Scorpio*

There is a strong emphasis now on broadening your horizons and on making sure you are in the right place at the right time to get ahead. Of course it's likely that not everyone will prove to be equally helpful today but if you turn in the right direction, you can be sure of the sort of support you are looking for.

2 WEDNESDAY *Moon Age Day 10 Moon Sign Sagittarius*

Domestic responsibilities could so easily get in the way of things you would rather be doing. It pays dividends to think in advance and to make sure all those chores are out of the way so that you can concentrate on having fun. Compliments could be coming your way from unlikely directions.

3 THURSDAY *Moon Age Day 11 Moon Sign Sagittarius*

Conversations of all kinds should be appealing today. When they involve matters at work, you should be able to utilise them to get ahead in a very positive manner. There is quite a restless streak about you now and there is no doubt that there are times you would rather be travelling than staying around to attend to responsibilities.

4 FRIDAY *Moon Age Day 12 Moon Sign Sagittarius*

Your powers of attraction should be stronger than ever today. Compliments come from a host of different directions but nothing being said is likely to turn your steady Capricorn head. Your intuition is strong, so you definitely know when someone is stringing you along, which could happen at this time.

5 SATURDAY *Moon Age Day 13 Moon Sign Capricorn*

The lunar high brings one of the best times during August. In today's bigger undertakings you should discover that good luck is on your side, and that things just seem to fall into place. Getting your own way if you are involved in group or teamwork should be especially easy and remains so for a few days.

6 SUNDAY *Moon Age Day 14 Moon Sign Capricorn*

Press on with whatever activities you have planned and assume that things are going to work out the way you would wish. In the main, this is likely to be the case. This could be the best day of all for financial ventures and is also a notable period in terms of your overall popularity. Just about anything you take on should go well now.

7 MONDAY *Moon Age Day 15 Moon Sign Aquarius*

The present position of the Sun allows you to come to terms with situations from the past, which could have a positive bearing on the way you are viewing the present. Take the opportunity to talk things through with a friend or relative if you get the chance. Friendly, and anxious to mix as much as possible, your social life should be particularly eventful now.

8 TUESDAY *Moon Age Day 16 Moon Sign Aquarius*

There are many changes around just now and your greatest desire is to keep life on an even keel. Actually, it could be the case that you are trying too hard. Allow things to happen in their own good time. If you are constantly reacting as soon as a subject is broached, it is possible that you are not using either your intuition or your common sense.

9 WEDNESDAY *Moon Age Day 17 Moon Sign Pisces*

Keep on looking for those wide, open spaces. This is a holiday time generally but turns out to be an especially good time for you to take a break. If you cannot get away from the rat race, at least leave some time free at some stage during the day. Even a walk in the park would be better than nothing.

10 THURSDAY *Moon Age Day 18 Moon Sign Pisces*

Your assertive nature now starts to show. This will come as a genuine surprise to some people and might be just what you need to wrong-foot the opposition. You won't take kindly to being told what to do, particularly in situations where you know you should be in the driving seat and will seize any chance you get to take control.

11 FRIDAY *Moon Age Day 19 Moon Sign Pisces*

This could be the high point of the month concerning travel and will see many Capricorns packing their bags and jetting off somewhere or other. It doesn't really matter how near or how far you go. The important thing is that you have worked hard of late and could certainly do with a change of pace.

12 SATURDAY *Moon Age Day 20 Moon Sign Aries*

A long-standing commitment could need urgent attention today. There is plenty on your agenda now but if you spread your commitments a little or even offload one or two of them on to willing volunteers, you should find the going easier. There are also positive financial influences around that can be exploited.

13 SUNDAY ☿ *Moon Age Day 21 Moon Sign Aries*

Your sense of self-importance is bound up in your opinions today and the two situations cannot really be separated. This is why you are less than willing to give ground with issues in which you have already reached conclusions. Capricorn also shows itself to be extremely creative in a number of ways today.

14 MONDAY ☿ *Moon Age Day 22 Moon Sign Taurus*

Any escape you want to make today could be either outwards or inwards. Some Capricorns are likely to have an introspective attitude towards the day and will be lost in their own dreams. The astrological circumstances today suggest you adopt whatever attitude suits you the best on a personal level.

15 TUESDAY ☿ *Moon Age Day 23 Moon Sign Taurus*

The emphasis falls on personal and domestic concerns today. Although there is still plenty going on in the outside world, you are taking less notice of it. Perhaps you want to set matters straight in a family sense or it could simply be that you realise how comfortable you are with life at home. This is never a bad thing so enjoy the atmosphere today.

16 WEDNESDAY ☿ *Moon Age Day 24 Moon Sign Gemini*

Right now the key to success seems to lie with your career. You may also need to deal with a few nagging details, even though these can prove to be quite tedious at times. Attention to matters of health might seem important but avoid worrying too much about situations that are not at all as they seem.

17 THURSDAY ☿ *Moon Age Day 25 Moon Sign Gemini*

An exchange of ideas and views could turn out to be very useful right now and there are plenty of people around who you could call on. In the end, probably the most unlikely person will end up being the one you go to, though you should definitely stay away from people who have difficulty enough keeping their own secrets, let alone yours.

18 FRIDAY ☿ *Moon Age Day 26 Moon Sign Cancer*

For perhaps one of the first times so far this month, the pace of life is slower than you would wish. This is the legacy of the lunar low. There are good elements of this period, though. Your ability to view situations dispassionately is very good and you would be unlikely to make any unforced errors.

19 SATURDAY ☿ *Moon Age Day 27 Moon Sign Cancer*

Things are still not likely to be moving quite a fast as you would wish, a fact that could lead to some small frustrations as the day wears on. Keep your eye on the ball, particularly if you are at work and don't allow others to steal a march on you. Your generally steady approach to life is an advantage.

20 SUNDAY ☿ *Moon Age Day 28 Moon Sign Leo*

The focus turns to leisure and pleasure and you clearly want to get as much fun from Sunday as you can. This extends to others because it is now very important for you to lift one or two people out of the doldrums. Your social conscience is strong and you are very charity-minded at the moment.

21 MONDAY ☿ *Moon Age Day 29 Moon Sign Leo*

Partnerships could turn out to be especially lucky at the moment. This may relate to personal attachments but is just as likely to be professional associations. Set out to have a good time today and talk as much as you can. It's plain that people are listening at the moment and that you are influencing them significantly.

22 TUESDAY ☿ *Moon Age Day 0 Moon Sign Virgo*

Keep a sense of proportion when you have to deal with people who seem determined to be awkward and learn that there is humour, even in the grumpy ways of certain people. There should be a good deal of emphasis on the fun side of life now and this part of the working week offers opportunities for diversion.

23 WEDNESDAY ☿ *Moon Age Day 1 Moon Sign Virgo*

Stay away from people who want to complicate situations and take the surest path you can through any job you become involved in. Be prepared for a little romance to enter your life before the day is out. This might turn out to be the case whether you are looking for love or not at the present time.

24 THURSDAY ☿ *Moon Age Day 2 Moon Sign Virgo*

A period of minor gains in and around your life generally is showing itself now. Travel is on the cards for some and the fact that your finances could be somewhat stronger should be a help in this direction. You have been working very hard of late and it now looks as though you can start to reap the rewards.

25 FRIDAY ☿ *Moon Age Day 3 Moon Sign Libra*

The present Capricorn yearning for adventure and a change of scenery remains undiminished. Get whatever you have to do out of the way and then head for the hills. Even if this proves to be impossible there is nothing at all to prevent your mind from wandering. You are particularly sensitive and caring at the moment.

26 SATURDAY ☿ *Moon Age Day 4 Moon Sign Libra*

Planetary influences that have a bearing on your home life now begin to be felt. It is possible that you will be involved in some family discussions and perhaps also discussing something important with your partner. If you don't have a romantic partner at the moment, just keep your eyes open – you never know who will come along.

27 SUNDAY ☿ *Moon Age Day 5 Moon Sign Scorpio*

Joint affairs of any sort are well highlighted for today. Such trends are especially useful in terms of business but of course this might not be helpful to you on a Sunday. You will probably wish to spread your wings as much as possible during today and for the coming week, even if late August is not holiday time for you.

28 MONDAY ☿ *Moon Age Day 6 Moon Sign Scorpio*

Stay away from the arguments of others because you could so easily become involved in matters that are nothing to do with you and this would spoil your day. The more light-hearted you are, the better the day will be. If you approach life in this way you are sure to find something really funny to laugh at right now.

29 TUESDAY ☿ *Moon Age Day 7 Moon Sign Sagittarius*

Avoid being too critical of the way others are behaving because in similar circumstances you might not be able to do any better. Although give and take comes as second nature to you as a rule, this is not necessarily the way things are under present planetary influences. Patience is really necessary today.

30 WEDNESDAY ☿ *Moon Age Day 8 Moon Sign Sagittarius*

What you should be doing as much as possible today is relaxing. If there are difficulties in this direction you can put them right before very long. Socially speaking you may decide to branch out and make some interesting new friends in the very near future. You should have confidence when it matters the most.

31 THURSDAY ☿ *Moon Age Day 9 Moon Sign Sagittarius*

Don't be too down in the mouth simply because people don't automatically do what you would wish. There are gains to be made, even when times are so quiet and nobody knows this better than Capricorn. What you are really good at today is planning, and also having some low-key fun with a friend or two. Tomorrow speeds things up.

September 2017

1 FRIDAY ☿ *Moon Age Day 10 Moon Sign Capricorn*

A very rewarding social phase is now in operation. With the Moon in your own zodiac sign, you are getting on with a whole variety of different sorts of people. In new ventures it is vital that you keep a sense of proportion, even when people around you are failing to do so and use your skill for co-operation and negotiation to the full.

2 SATURDAY ☿ *Moon Age Day 11 Moon Sign Capricorn*

This is a day during which you should find it possible to talk anyone into doing anything you wish. Your influence is extremely strong at this time and this isn't just because of the lunar high. You have been gradually increasing your persuasive ways to such an extent that you will have even the most awkward types eating out of your hand.

3 SUNDAY ☿ *Moon Age Day 12 Moon Sign Aquarius*

You certainly intend to make yourself heard today and you won't be backward when it comes to letting people know what's on your mind. Do your best to make sure you don't offer any unintentional offence to anyone. The present position of Mars can take just a little of the recent charm out of your nature.

4 MONDAY ☿ *Moon Age Day 13 Moon Sign Aquarius*

It is in your professional life that things really tend to go with a swing now, though you can't dismiss the possibilities that also exist socially, and in romantic attachments. Capricorn is also quite willing to learn at the moment so perhaps you are developing a new interest or skill? If so, put all your energies into it.

5 TUESDAY ☿ *Moon Age Day 14 Moon Sign Aquarius*

You can't please all of the people all of the time, a saying that is likely to make real sense to you today. There are times when it is pointless trying and in the end all you can do is be certain you are doing your best. Some people might disbelieve even that – but that's just the way life is.

6 WEDNESDAY ☿ *Moon Age Day 15 Moon Sign Pisces*

You are probably making a greater impression on some people than you think. This is especially likely to be the case with those who are your intended romantic targets. Capricorn is not showy or particularly noisy but you can still let people know you are around. Your confidence is almost palpable today.

7 THURSDAY ☿ *Moon Age Day 16 Moon Sign Pisces*

Where communication is concerned, you have it within you to get the best from others today. You have a natural tendency at present to fight for the underdog but before you do make certain your support is justified in any specific case. There might be slightly more money around than you expected.

8 FRIDAY ☿ *Moon Age Day 17 Moon Sign Aries*

Things should still be going well at home, which is probably why you spend as much time there at the moment as you can. There could be a few jitters with regard to public appearances, especially if you are expected to speak to a large group of people. Don't worry, the planets are on your side and you'll do fine.

9 SATURDAY ☿ *Moon Age Day 18 Moon Sign Aries*

There are some potentially interesting encounters around during the weekend, though not of course if you insist on staying behind closed doors. Now you need to spread your wings and there are people around you who will be only too willing to take a trip somewhere special with you.

10 SUNDAY ☿ *Moon Age Day 19 Moon Sign Taurus*

This is a time when you will be asserting your independence and making it plain to almost anyone that you want to plough your own furrow. Although you may encounter some slight opposition to your plans right now, in the main your obvious determination will resign others to your chosen course of action.

11 MONDAY ☿ *Moon Age Day 20 Moon Sign Taurus*

The more variety you have in your life, the better you are likely to enjoy yourself today. The start of a new working week means scoring significantly more successes than was possible last week. Right from the start you need to enlist the support of people you know to have similar ideas to your own.

12 TUESDAY ☿ *Moon Age Day 21 Moon Sign Gemini*

You have plenty of opportunity at the moment to simply be yourself. You might think that the real you is not all that interesting or inspiring but it's what others think that counts. Show some caution in business dealings and don't allow anyone to fool you or you could lose out – possibly in financial terms.

13 WEDNESDAY *Moon Age Day 22 Moon Sign Gemini*

Work and practical matters could provide a few frustrations today. The fact is that you can't make things go the way you would wish and that won't please you at all. Your best area of today will be your social life, which offers a great deal in the way of enjoyment. Perhaps make some plans for the evening?

14 THURSDAY *Moon Age Day 23 Moon Sign Cancer*

It might be best to suspend major activities wherever you can, at least until Saturday. That means giving yourself more spare time, some of which you can spend building broken bridges, particularly in the family. The fact that not everyone is seeing eye to eye at present isn't your fault, but it might feel as if it is.

15 FRIDAY *Moon Age Day 24 Moon Sign Cancer*

This could be another slightly quieter day and definitely not one during which you should take any financial risks. Keep it light and steady, no matter what you decide to do. If there are parties going on somewhere in your vicinity, you will wish to join in, despite the fact that your social skills seem somewhat diminished at present.

16 SATURDAY *Moon Age Day 25 Moon Sign Cancer*

Don't be reluctant to ask even big favours from people whom you have helped significantly in the past because the chances are that they would be more than willing to put themselves out on your behalf. Friends and family alike prove to be very entertaining today and have the ability to lift your spirits no end.

17 SUNDAY *Moon Age Day 26 Moon Sign Leo*

Trends move on and you may now find it more difficult to make compromises than it has been at any time so far this month. This is probably because you are coming to terms with people you either do not like or respect. Capricorns are usually friendly and always fair – but they don't suffer fools gladly.

18 MONDAY *Moon Age Day 27 Moon Sign Leo*

Don't put off until tomorrow anything that you know in your heart you can complete easily now. Once again you will discover that everyday routines are not all that interesting, though even these can be undertaken with a smile if you put your mind to it. Romance could brighten the new week before today is out.

19 TUESDAY *Moon Age Day 28 Moon Sign Virgo*

The force of your personality appears powerful now and people really do listen to what you have to say – which is a great deal more than usual. It is your practical skills that always win out in the end, together with that famous Capricorn intelligence. Even if you are young in years it becomes obvious today that you are old in terms of wisdom.

20 WEDNESDAY *Moon Age Day 0 Moon Sign Virgo*

Your ideas and even what might once have seemed your most outrageous schemes can find good support from others today. This is partly because you are explaining yourself so well and you won't have any difficulty persuading people that you know what you are talking about. Keep abreast of current affairs.

21 THURSDAY *Moon Age Day 1 Moon Sign Libra*

The main accent is now on your home life and private concerns and considerations. Although you are still in a position to have fun, you might be taking life a little more seriously than you have done for the last few days. Anything odd, old or unusual could have a particular appeal for you under present trends.

22 FRIDAY *Moon Age Day 2 Moon Sign Libra*

You have quite strong views all of the time, but you don't show them all that often. This is something that sets you apart right now because you are more outspoken than would usually be the case. You know what you want from life and quite a few people are going to discover the fact in the near future.

23 SATURDAY *Moon Age Day 3 Moon Sign Scorpio*

Expressing your feelings might not be a smooth process today. Capricorn is now somewhat prickly and inclined to take offence when none is intended. This isn't a long-term problem and it need not have a bearing on your life at all if you recognise the signs. Try to relax because there is no point in being tense.

24 SUNDAY *Moon Age Day 4 Moon Sign Scorpio*

Along comes a high point in your social calendar, which also brings more invitations and possibilities for fun. Sunday should work out quite well for you and is likely to be split between activity today and a more restful approach later. The confidence to say what is really on your mind is likely to be present now.

25 MONDAY *Moon Age Day 5 Moon Sign Scorpio*

Your sense of personal security is as important now as it ever gets to you. If you were a medieval monarch, you would now be opening all your treasure chests and counting the gold pieces. As it is, you are likely to throw your attentions into making sure that all details are sorted and that your path ahead is unobstructed.

26 TUESDAY *Moon Age Day 6 Moon Sign Sagittarius*

It is now easy for you to work with those who are in any sort of position of authority and you could even find that more responsibility is coming your way in the very near future. Not everyone seems to have your best interests at heart and it is just possible that an acquaintance will be exposed as some sort of impostor around now.

27 WEDNESDAY *Moon Age Day 7 Moon Sign Sagittarius*

The focus is now definitely on your public persona and even if you don't really feel like it there is a distinct possibility that you will be in the spotlight today. This can make you feel rather vulnerable but is good for you in terms of confidence building. Look for a fun Wednesday and a chance to mix with valued friends.

28 THURSDAY *Moon Age Day 8 Moon Sign Capricorn*

Today should start with a flourish as the Moon moves into your zodiac sign. Since things have been slower of late, the position of the Moon should come as something of a revelation to you. It allows you to get ahead in a general sense but also ensures you will be conscious of the popularity that you might have felt was missing.

29 FRIDAY *Moon Age Day 9 Moon Sign Capricorn*

You can certainly afford to be more ambitious with your plans today and should not fail to promote yourself at every opportunity. Good luck seems to be on your side but there's more to it than this. You are in a romantic mood with your partner and will be charming everyone you come across in a social and a personal sense.

30 SATURDAY *Moon Age Day 10 Moon Sign Capricorn*

What you need most of all today is keep an optimistic and positive outlook. Don't allow yourself to be stifled by the opinions of people you are not naturally drawn to. You may find that, in a practical sense, it is not easy to get things done. If so, don't let this worry you as a smooth-running interval is just around the corner.

October

2017

1 SUNDAY *Moon Age Day 11 Moon Sign Aquarius*

This is the time to ditch whatever has been holding you back. If this is going to prove awkward or embarrassing, you might have to think things through first. What you can't do is carry on down a road that definitely isn't the right one for you. Comfort and security mean a great deal by the evening.

2 MONDAY *Moon Age Day 12 Moon Sign Aquarius*

Your sense of adventure is strong this Monday. You almost certainly will not want to stay at home and put your feet up. This is the sort of period during which you set yourself a challenge and then go out and win. Advice from others is well intentioned but you probably don't want it and prefer to follow your own course.

3 TUESDAY *Moon Age Day 13 Moon Sign Pisces*

It's time to get busy. With energy levels particularly high and a genuine desire to get things done, you can probably start very early in the day. Once the practical necessities of the day are sorted it's time to go out and have fun. You probably won't stop moving from the time you wake up until the moment you go to bed again.

4 WEDNESDAY *Moon Age Day 14 Moon Sign Pisces*

Relationships of almost any sort can be emotionally uplifting but where love and romance are concerned, the world should be your oyster right now. Your confidence is not lacking, though it is higher in personal rather than professional situations. You could be on the receiving end of a very special favour.

5 THURSDAY *Moon Age Day 15 Moon Sign Aries*

You can't believe everything you hear today, even if in a few cases you wish you could. A good dose of scepticism might prove to be necessary because there are some tall tales around. Just when you think everyone is talking nonsense, though, the silliest story of all might just turn out to be true.

6 FRIDAY *Moon Age Day 16 Moon Sign Aries*

You may feel as though travel plans are something you want to think about today. If you have any journey planned in the very near future, make very sure that you have all the details sorted out well in advance. Small disagreements with your partner, or family members, shouldn't be taken out of proportion.

7 SATURDAY *Moon Age Day 17 Moon Sign Taurus*

You probably devoted yesterday to practical issues and so today is, quite reasonably, a period you can spend on yourself. Seek out a little luxury and pamper yourself. If there are issues concerning your home or personal life that you have shied away from in the past, now is the time to tackle them head on.

8 SUNDAY *Moon Age Day 18 Moon Sign Taurus*

Today you may be introduced to some inspirational people, and it is possible that they might make you look at life in a radically new and different way. Although your own thinking right now probably could not be considered inspirational, you do have a good ability to see clearly to the heart of things, which itself can be a great help.

9 MONDAY *Moon Age Day 19 Moon Sign Taurus*

Do whatever you can to bring out the sunny side of your nature today. There are strong planetary influences causing you to look at things in a very positive way and which only require a small push from you to become quite powerful. One thing you certainly won't lack is general popularity.

10 TUESDAY *Moon Age Day 20 Moon Sign Gemini*

A long-standing commitment can be addressed at this stage of October. Get it out of the way as quickly as you can because what matters is leaving yourself free to do the things that come upon you quickly. Negotiating your path through a pile of red tape might not help but you are equal enough to the task.

11 WEDNESDAY *Moon Age Day 21 Moon Sign Gemini*

If there are any restrictions placed on you personally today, you are likely to feel very frustrated and annoyed. The truth is that Capricorn knows where it wants to go and won't take kindly to being prevented from doing so. All the same, you retain the essential popularity that is your usual lot.

12 THURSDAY *Moon Age Day 22 Moon Sign Cancer*

It might be best to allow others to take some of the decisions, at least whilst the lunar low is around. It won't be easy to make any real progress and you may find that you need the advice and support that others can offer in order to make the very best of the day. The main problem is that everything seems to take so long.

13 FRIDAY *Moon Age Day 23 Moon Sign Cancer*

Your general capabilities are not up to scratch, or at least that's the way it seems from your perspective. Actually, you are probably doing a great deal better than you realise. Towards the end of the day, you should discover that things are brightening up generally but don't take any undue risks all the same.

14 SATURDAY *Moon Age Day 24 Moon Sign Leo*

You show great efficiency today and can be sure that whatever you tackle gets done well and quickly. Don't be at all surprised if your popularity is going off the scale and make the most of the improving social trends. There are some very talkative people around at the moment and you are not the least of them.

15 SUNDAY *Moon Age Day 25 Moon Sign Leo*

The desire you are presently feeling to broaden your horizons can prove to be a very good incentive at this time. Few situations should be holding you back, though you are likely to find some difficulty with younger family members, wayward friends and possibly a person who constantly embarrasses you.

16 MONDAY *Moon Age Day 26 Moon Sign Virgo*

You know how to enjoy yourself and will be so flexible in your attitude at the moment that some people won't really recognise you at all. Winning others round to your point of view ought to be easy and there are gains to be made simply from looking at life with such a wonderful sense of humour as you presently enjoy.

17 TUESDAY *Moon Age Day 27 Moon Sign Virgo*

Today you will be dynamic, expressive and quite magnetic. If you want to get your own way, this is the single most important day during October to do so. You may have a concern that you are being rather too assertive for your own good, as you feel well and truly in the spotlight but on balance you will probably decide that it was worthwhile.

18 WEDNESDAY *Moon Age Day 28 Moon Sign Libra*

Although you are getting along well with others at this time it might be necessary to stand in the background now and again. Although this might not bother you much, there are going to be times when you know much better than the people who take the lead. Simply grin and wait for your time to come.

19 THURSDAY *Moon Age Day 29 Moon Sign Libra*

There is nothing at all to prevent you from pitching in and having a go now, no matter what it is you want to do. Your confidence works in your favour and people really believe in your abilities. There are some attractive individuals around at the moment and you will be doing almost anything you can to please the ones you care about the most.

20 FRIDAY *Moon Age Day 0 Moon Sign Libra*

One-to-one relationships could seem to have a few drawbacks today and perhaps even over the coming weekend. The best way to deal with this situation is to mix more freely with a number of different people. Don't allow yourself to be restricted by pointless red tape or by rules and regulations you simply do not understand.

21 SATURDAY *Moon Age Day 1 Moon Sign Scorpio*

You might find yourself rather alone when it comes to pressing ahead in quite the way you would wish. This is a very temporary situation and not one that will trouble you all that much in any case. Your partner should be able to provide a sense of emotional security, which is what matters most at present.

22 SUNDAY *Moon Age Day 2 Moon Sign Scorpio*

The opportunities for gains of all sorts are many during this Sunday. Whether or not you intend to exploit them your Capricorn abilities are on display. Arrangements for journeys may have to be altered but the results might turn out to be the better than your original plans. People are keen to listen to your point of view at this time.

23 MONDAY *Moon Age Day 3 Moon Sign Sagittarius*

Someone could be throwing their weight around today, a situation that you will not be willing to tolerate. You need to let any such person know how you feel and that will probably be enough to remedy the situation. From the perspective of others you appear to be both confident and very determined.

24 TUESDAY *Moon Age Day 4 Moon Sign Sagittarius*

Your imagination is likely to be working overtime, which has good and bad repercussions. You can imagine all sorts of monsters but none of them has any substance whatsoever. If you feel the weight of certain worries, tackle them one at a time and with the help of people who are in the know.

25 WEDNESDAY *Moon Age Day 5 Moon Sign Sagittarius*

There are some extremely positive romantic trends building in your solar chart. All the same, there are also some frustrations around, probably rising to the surface as a result of painful memories. You need to tell yourself that the past is over and done with. The future is what matters so do some planning for it now.

26 THURSDAY *Moon Age Day 6 Moon Sign Capricorn*

The lunar high for this month carries a promise of better luck and an ability to see through what might look like the fog of life, clear to the heart of situations. You know what you want from life at the moment and have a fairly good idea how you are going to get it. Set out your stall for others to see and make the most of the positive trends.

27 FRIDAY *Moon Age Day 7 Moon Sign Capricorn*

The profile you have when in company is quite high at present, leading you into taking a few chances that you would shy away from under normal circumstances. Where there have been problems in your life, you tend to address them one at a time and in this way could soon demolish a whole pile of minor concerns.

28 SATURDAY *Moon Age Day 8 Moon Sign Aquarius*

Your social life and group ventures generally are important this weekend and you should do everything within your power in order to enjoy yourself as much as you can. Make the weekend your own by getting out of the house with relatives or friends and by seeking to push the bounds of the possible.

29 SUNDAY *Moon Age Day 9 Moon Sign Aquarius*

Friends should be very supportive and extremely loyal at this time. It won't be hard for you to trust people and you can rely on your intuition when it comes to sorting out the wheat from the chaff. There are gains to be made on the financial front but you will need to be careful about investing large sums of money.

30 MONDAY *Moon Age Day 10 Moon Sign Pisces*

With such a large focus on professional matters it is almost certain that you are making a good impression at work right now. Those Capricorns who are between positions should be looking even more closely today for the right opportunity. Help can come from some very surprising directions.

31 TUESDAY *Moon Age Day 11 Moon Sign Pisces*

You are now highly susceptible to outside influences but most of them will be potentially positive around this time. Some confusion is possible, particularly when you don't listen carefully to what family members or your partner are saying. This would not be the best time to gamble or to ignore what you know to be good advice.

November
2017

1 WEDNESDAY *Moon Age Day 12 Moon Sign Pisces*

Perhaps you need to move swiftly with plans and duties today. There are things that need doing and some of them can only be done by you. However, don't confuse this fact with a sense that the world can't cope without you. A balanced view is necessary and you are just the person to take one.

2 THURSDAY *Moon Age Day 13 Moon Sign Aries*

Today should be very enjoyable from a social point of view, even if you can't get everything you want in a material sense. In a way, that won't matter because the most important gifts that come to you now cost nothing in monetary terms. Putting a price on love, respect and genuine affection is impossible.

3 FRIDAY *Moon Age Day 14 Moon Sign Aries*

When it comes to making decisions at the moment, you can't take anything for granted. Look at situations carefully and maybe take some advice from people in the know. Generally speaking, you want to enjoy what this Friday has to offer, most likely in the company of your partner or a good friend.

4 SATURDAY *Moon Age Day 15 Moon Sign Taurus*

Friendly co-operation is on the cards for today. If you are working today, join forces with colleagues and you can gain a great deal more than you would by going it alone. Your creative potential remains good and it is also possible that you are choosing this time to make some changes in and around your home.

5 SUNDAY *Moon Age Day 16 Moon Sign Taurus*

Look out for a helpful period during which just about anyone you meet wants to offer the sort of help and support that is really useful. Don't let your recent desire to do everything yourself get in the way of accepting a little assistance. If you do, there's a good chance you will upset someone who is important to you.

6 MONDAY *Moon Age Day 17 Moon Sign Gemini*

Getting to grips with facts and figures might not be very inviting today but it could be necessary all the same. There are jobs to do that you really don't want to tackle, but in the end you do them with good grace, probably early in the day, if only to get them out of the way so that you can have fun.

7 TUESDAY *Moon Age Day 18 Moon Sign Gemini*

There are many good things likely to happen around you today, not least of all in career matters. Although this is an area of life that can take up a good deal of time, it probably isn't the most important sphere. In the end it is relationships that will capture your imagination the most so make sure to put time aside for them.

8 WEDNESDAY *Moon Age Day 19 Moon Sign Cancer*

A fairly sluggish day is on the cards and a time when it might be difficult to get what you want from situations. To a great extent, you can blame the arrival of the lunar low. What won't help is to push on against all the odds. It would be far better to take a rest and come out fighting in a couple of days.

9 THURSDAY *Moon Age Day 20 Moon Sign Cancer*

This is another day on which it will be impossible to get your own way in everything. Simply watch and wait, biding your time and laying down plans that you can put into action as soon as tomorrow arrives. Your confidence might seem to be lacking at present but, again, this is only a very temporary glitch.

10 FRIDAY *Moon Age Day 21 Moon Sign Leo*

Clear communication will be essential if you want to enjoy a successful life at the end of this working week. Make sure others know perfectly well what you are saying, and why. On another front you might notice that there are many personal compliments coming your way, perhaps from interesting directions.

11 SATURDAY *Moon Age Day 22 Moon Sign Leo*

You can probably look forward to a little ego boost in social encounters because more compliments are likely to be coming your way. Under present circumstances this situation is hardly likely to turn you head but it is good to know that people notice you and want to be pleasant.

12 SUNDAY *Moon Age Day 23 Moon Sign Virgo*

Throw negative thinking straight into a wastebasket and get on with living your life as positively as you can. Rules and regulations are almost certain to get on your nerves, even if you were originally responsible for instigating some of them yourself. It is really important that you find ways to enjoy this Sunday.

13 MONDAY *Moon Age Day 24 Moon Sign Virgo*

Trends suggest that compromises don't come easily to you now and you will have to try that little bit harder to deal with behaviour and attitudes you don't entirely understand. What you can be sure of today is that the future looks generally brighter and that you are now socialising more than of late.

14 TUESDAY *Moon Age Day 25 Moon Sign Libra*

This is likely to be a socially favourable day and one during which you can enhance your financial wherewithal, simply by saying and doing the right things. Don't get stuck on specifics because it is the broad cross-section of life that matters at the moment. It might have occurred to you for the first time today that Christmas is not really too far away.

15 WEDNESDAY *Moon Age Day 26 Moon Sign Libra*

You have some ingenious methods for getting ahead right now and can make the most of even little opportunities that come your way. Although you find yourself somewhat frustrated by the attitude or opinions of particular friends, you are wise enough to know there are reasons for this strange behaviour.

16 THURSDAY *Moon Age Day 27 Moon Sign Libra*

Your strengths and personal resources are now improving noticeably. There are some benefactors about and even though these might not be the people you would expect, they are worth your attention. Not everything that leads to a sense of personal success can be measured in financial terms right now.

17 FRIDAY *Moon Age Day 28 Moon Sign Scorpio*

Although you are still pushing forward progressively, this is not a day during which you should allow your ego to get in the way. You need to remain fixed in your basic attitude yet still flexible enough to bend with the wind. Someone you don't see very often could be making a return visit to your life.

18 SATURDAY *Moon Age Day 0 Moon Sign Scorpio*

There are signs of new romantic developments on the way for at least some sons and daughters of Capricorn. If you have been on the lookout for new love, this is a time when it could easily come along. Don't be too fixed in your attitude as far as work is concerned and be prepared to learn from those who are in the know.

19 SUNDAY *Moon Age Day 1 Moon Sign Sagittarius*

Although today should be generally settled, there could be some romantic tension about and this is something you would like to avoid if at all possible. Give yourself time to relax, even though some practical matters might be pressing in on you. Above all, remember this is Sunday, which is supposed to be a day of rest.

20 MONDAY *Moon Age Day 2 Moon Sign Sagittarius*

A selfish streak comes upon Capricorn, which isn't at all typical of your zodiac sign. Try to keep it in check but at the same time realise that you can move forward as a result. In just about every sphere of your life the day is predominantly about balance and you need to be sure that you understand this and capitalise on it.

21 TUESDAY *Moon Age Day 3 Moon Sign Sagittarius*

Get routine jobs done as early in the day as you can, leaving you with more time later to have fun and to get on with the newest incentives that are coming into your life. Your confidence remains generally high so you should not hang back in any situation and you have it within you to really make the day go with a swing.

22 WEDNESDAY *Moon Age Day 4 Moon Sign Capricorn*

This is the time when you really need to go out on a limb to get what you want from life. There is any number of potential opportunities coming along and with the lunar high giving you that extra oomph, no other planetary influence will get in the way. Don't be held back when you know what you are talking about.

23 THURSDAY *Moon Age Day 5 Moon Sign Capricorn*

Your confidence is greatly increased and there isn't much doubt about your desire to get ahead. This may not be easy in a professional sense at first but you are very good at mixing business with pleasure at this time. Ideal situations might just happen by themselves but a little push from you won't do any harm either.

24 FRIDAY *Moon Age Day 6 Moon Sign Aquarius*

After the lunar high it may be a good idea to suspend any major decisions for the moment and to opt instead for a quiet time and a period during which you can bask in the love that is coming your way, particularly from family members. By tomorrow you will want to act positively again but for the moment you need to relax.

25 SATURDAY *Moon Age Day 7 Moon Sign Aquarius*

A loved one or a family member requires fairly careful handling today, especially if they have recently had something of a rough ride. You will be in a good position to offer them a guiding hand. For your own part you are now definitely in the mood for fun and should know where to find it.

26 SUNDAY *Moon Age Day 8 Moon Sign Aquarius*

There are serious considerations to be taken on board now and this would not be a particularly good time to think of new business deals or signing documents when you haven't read the small print. There are gains to be made but these are generally likely to be of a personal rather than a practical nature.

27 MONDAY *Moon Age Day 9 Moon Sign Pisces*

Participation in group events gives today an air of excitement and it is very easy for you to join in and have fun. Not everyone appears to have your best interests at heart but it is possible that in a few cases you are misinterpreting the situation. A better day for finances is possible with perhaps some unexpected gains.

28 TUESDAY *Moon Age Day 10 Moon Sign Pisces*

It is highly likely now that a little good luck could come from the direction of friendships. You just can't get enough of your pals at the moment and will trust them implicitly. There are gains to be made as a result of efforts you made in the past and some interesting communications could also be coming your way at any time now.

29 WEDNESDAY *Moon Age Day 11 Moon Sign Aries*

Any intellectual work is now highly rewarding and communication is well highlighted in your solar chart. Both your mind and your heart can be stimulated through new ideas and you are well able to offer good guidance to both associates and friends. Something you hear might confirm your suspicions regarding a colleague or acquaintance.

30 THURSDAY *Moon Age Day 12 Moon Sign Aries*

Travel could be uppermost in your mind and if you are planning a long journey it might be sensible to speak to someone who knows the location well. Check and recheck all details before you embark. This is the best time of the week for conversation, even with people you have never met before.

December 2017

1 FRIDAY *Moon Age Day 13 Moon Sign Taurus*

The main thing today is keeping on top of organisational issues. You won't be very pleased with yourself if situations become confused or if you are not keeping up with the expectations others have of you. In a more general sense, you ought to be feeling quite positive about life.

2 SATURDAY *Moon Age Day 14 Moon Sign Taurus*

The spirit of teamwork is stronger in you today and your ability to get on well with the world at large is more noticeable. Specific planetary trends show this to be a time during which Capricorn becomes fascinated by the way things work. Some experimentation may be called for, if only to satisfy your curiosity.

3 SUNDAY ☿ *Moon Age Day 15 Moon Sign Gemini*

Teamwork remains rewarding and it looks as though you are becoming the life and soul of any party you can find. Active and inspirational, you respond very well to changing circumstances and will now be more willing to actually encourage a small degree of uncertainty and even risk to come into your life. This might not be you usual way, but it could pay dividends now.

4 MONDAY ☿ *Moon Age Day 16 Moon Sign Gemini*

Although friends could have a confused attitude towards specific situations, your own mind is crystal clear and you have little or no difficulty in organising yourself and others. The social whirl of Christmas might have started for you already, which would be no bad thing when you are feeling so positive.

5 TUESDAY ☿ *Moon Age Day 17 Moon Sign Cancer*

Things change quickly. Let's face it, this is not your luckiest period, even though gains can come along as a result of past efforts. Take life steadily and rely on the good offices of people who have never failed to help you out in the past. Improvements should come from all manner of directions in a couple of days.

6 WEDNESDAY ☿ *Moon Age Day 18 Moon Sign Cancer*

You are still trying very hard to swim against a tide that really will not turn in your favour. Maybe it should have occurred to you by now that this is a complete waste of time and effort. Let someone else take the strain for the moment, while you sit back and enjoy yourself. Capricorn can rest with a very clear conscience now.

7 THURSDAY ☿ *Moon Age Day 19 Moon Sign Leo*

Gathering together all the relevant information you need should be child's play now. You are particularly well organised at the moment, which is probably why others turn to you when they need sorting out. It might be necessary to fend off one or two social invitations, if only because you can't do everything.

8 FRIDAY ☿ *Moon Age Day 20 Moon Sign Leo*

Avoid potentially deceptive situations if at all possible this Friday. If you are about to sign a document, read the details very carefully. It isn't often that Capricorn is duped or fooled and once you realise that this is a possibility today you will be on your guard. Interaction with some family members might make you laugh.

9 SATURDAY ☿ *Moon Age Day 21 Moon Sign Virgo*

Your energy is not unlimited at the moment so you will have to move somewhat carefully. Concentrate on those jobs you know to be the most important and pace yourself, especially during the first part of the day. You should not have any difficulty finding sufficient reserves for social functions later.

10 SUNDAY ☿ *Moon Age Day 22 Moon Sign Virgo*

Certain sacrifices will have to be made today if you want to get the very best out of any relationship. Although there are things you want to do, now may not be the right time to address them. You are spreading yourself quite thinly already and could probably do with offloading unnecessary tasks or information.

11 MONDAY ☿ *Moon Age Day 23 Moon Sign Virgo*

Career developments should now be going your way, though on a day that has much to recommend it in terms of sociability and general happenings, work could be the last thing on your mind. Find some time for both today, as even casual conversations with others may lead you to far-reaching conclusions.

12 TUESDAY ☿ *Moon Age Day 24 Moon Sign Libra*

You are likely to be occupying a centre-stage position right now and should be very willing to entertain others. This might not be what Capricorn is about as a rule but you do have it within you now to be extremely showy. At heart, you are still as keen to look after your own life and circumstances as is always the case.

13 WEDNESDAY ☿ *Moon Age Day 25 Moon Sign Libra*

Some unusual planetary trends now mean that you should excel as a social being and benefit from all kinds of activities that involve others. This is so different from the way Capricorn sometimes is that you may surprise yourself. You also have it within you to be lucky in love right now. A new relationship could be on the horizon for some.

14 THURSDAY ☿ *Moon Age Day 26 Moon Sign Scorpio*

You do well when you are in the limelight and when involved in any sort of group activity. It could be that Christmas has come early to Capricorn or merely that the present planetary trends are encouraging you towards ever more social tendencies. These are also good trends in which to feather your own nest professionally.

15 FRIDAY ☿ *Moon Age Day 27 Moon Sign Scorpio*

Make sure you explain yourself properly early in the day to avoid others getting the wrong end of the stick. Clear communication is the key and can avoid you being disappointed by the outcome of any encounter. Business matters are now variable but in any case you might have other things on your mind.

16 SATURDAY ☿ *Moon Age Day 28 Moon Sign Scorpio*

You might have to sacrifice your own interests a little this Saturday, in favour of thinking about the group. This could be family or it may be your friends but there is no doubt that you are very generous in your feelings and actions now. There are contrasts around you, not least of all in the way others behave.

17 SUNDAY ☿ *Moon Age Day 29 Moon Sign Sagittarius*

A great deal of what you do today could seem to be more trouble than it is worth. As a result you might decide that the time is right for a one-day holiday. That might be difficult because there are still things to be done before Christmas comes along. Don't worry, you will feel more like taking part tomorrow.

18 MONDAY ☿ *Moon Age Day 0 Moon Sign Sagittarius*

Differences of opinion are likely to crop up now and there probably isn't very much you can do about it. What you can do, however, is to ignore people you don't particularly like very much, rather than reacting adversely to them. Routines can be tedious right now and if this proves to be the case, find ways to sidestep them.

19 TUESDAY ☿ *Moon Age Day 1 Moon Sign Capricorn*

As the month advances, so you begin to realise with startling clarity that Christmas will soon be here. That won't be any problem today or tomorrow because you have more than enough energy to organise things. The lunar high makes you feel very positive about most situations now.

20 WEDNESDAY ☿ *Moon Age Day 2 Moon Sign Capricorn*

This is a high point in the month during which you are turning your attention towards plans you have wanted to put into action for some time. Your general level of energy is high and a little good luck attends many of your efforts. Act now in order to reap the maximum benefit in the days and weeks to come.

21 THURSDAY ☿ *Moon Age Day 3 Moon Sign Capricorn*

Trends place a strong emphasis on independence, bringing you a certain desire to do things your own way. That's fine unless you are in a position that means you have no choice but to co-operate with others. In the end, though, it may turn out that your ideas are the best and if you use a little psychology you can get other people to think so too.

22 FRIDAY ☿ *Moon Age Day 4 Moon Sign Aquarius*

Your personal charm really comes to the fore and with Christmas only a few days away you should be able to create a positively magical setting, particularly for younger people. Rewards might come along as a result of decisions and actions you took in the past, perhaps putting your finances on a firmer footing.

23 SATURDAY *Moon Age Day 5 Moon Sign Aquarius*

Advice is likely to be forthcoming from a number of different directions today, even if you haven't been looking for it at all. You might have to bite your tongue, especially when people are telling you things you already know. Don't let this worry you, you can be quite diplomatic when the mood takes you.

24 SUNDAY *Moon Age Day 6 Moon Sign Pisces*

It's Christmas Eve, a fact that could so easily take you more or less by surprise. You have been so busy dealing with the practical aspects of life that you might have forgotten about the celebrations altogether! You will soon make up for any deficiency and should enjoy a very family-motivated sort of day.

25 MONDAY *Moon Age Day 7 Moon Sign Pisces*

You should be in for a very interesting and varied sort of Christmas Day. It could be that not everyone in your family and friendship circle is having quite as good a time as you are and this could mean that the focus is on you to put in some extra effort. The most enjoyable associations today come via close, personal attachments.

26 TUESDAY *Moon Age Day 8 Moon Sign Pisces*

Capricorn is inclined to have a liking for the good life, as do all Earth signs, but when the need arises you are usually able to get along quite well with just the basics. What seems to matter to you most right now is the affection that comes from family members. All the same, if you have expensive tastes you might get the opportunity to indulge them.

27 WEDNESDAY *Moon Age Day 9 Moon Sign Aries*

There should be plenty of opportunities to help others today, even if the truth is that you would rather please yourself. The Sun has now entered your solar first house, one of the best planetary trends when it comes to feathering your own nest. It also improves your sociability and causes you to be chatty and friendly.

28 THURSDAY *Moon Age Day 10 Moon Sign Aries*

Your social life and friendships seem to receive the best planetary support now, meaning that you could be taking the opportunity to see people you don't get the chance to meet up with very often. There are good trends around supporting the possibility of travel and you could easily get itchy feet if you spend too long in front of the television.

29 FRIDAY *Moon Age Day 11 Moon Sign Taurus*

There are gains coming from very unlikely directions and before today is out the hint that things are looking up generally. You won't be at all shy when it comes to singing your own praises and will be generally popular with all sorts of people. You can't keep a good Capricorn down, especially not right now.

30 SATURDAY *Moon Age Day 12 Moon Sign Taurus*

It is possible that you will be saying some things you don't really mean when involved in a romantic encounter. The Goat has a tendency to be a little outspoken today, so watch out for this and try to curb it if you can. Consideration is usually your forte but everyone has off days. Try to include someone who is lonely in your arrangements.

31 SUNDAY *Moon Age Day 13 Moon Sign Gemini*

Get out and about as much as possible and certainly aim to have a really good time tonight. As for New Year resolutions, it might be best to leave them on the shelf for the moment. You will think more clearly about them once January actually arrives. Encounters with others may inspire some new ideas.

RISING SIGNS FOR CAPRICORN

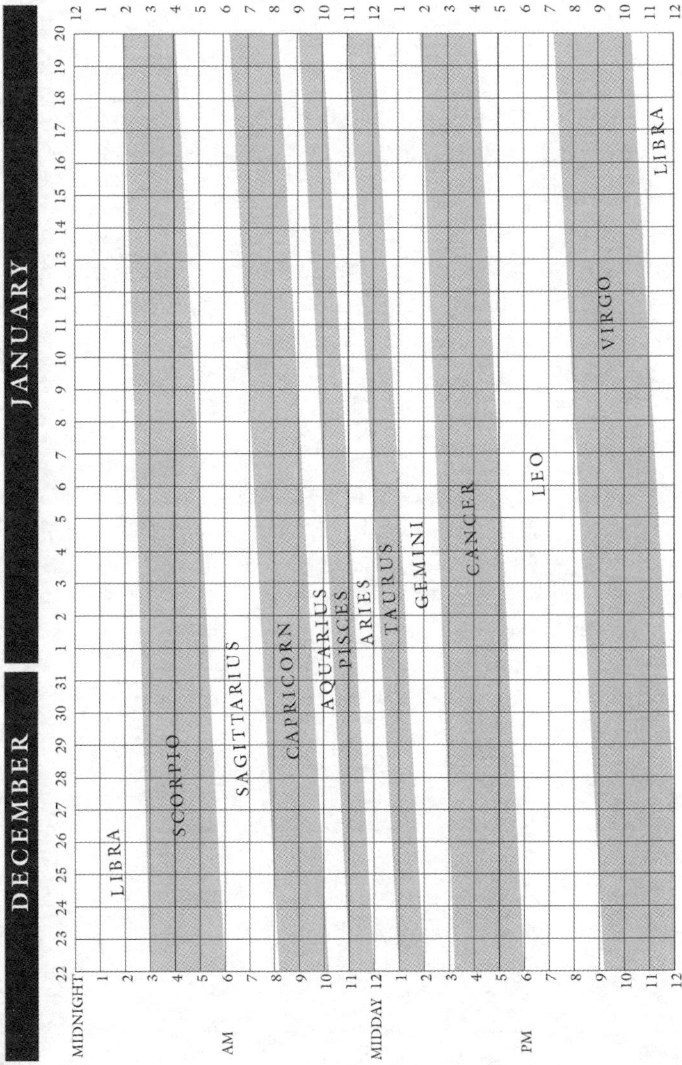

THE ZODIAC, PLANETS AND CORRESPONDENCES

The Earth revolves around the Sun once every calendar year, so when viewed from Earth the Sun appears in a different part of the sky as the year progresses. In astrology, these parts of the sky are divided into the signs of the zodiac and this means that the signs are organised in a circle. The circle begins with Aries and ends with Pisces.

Taking the zodiac sign as a starting point, astrologers then work with all the positions of planets, stars and many other factors to calculate horoscopes and birth charts and tell us what the stars have in store for us.

The table below shows the planets and Elements for each of the signs of the zodiac. Each sign belongs to one of the four Elements: Fire, Air, Earth or Water. Fire signs are creative and enthusiastic; Air signs are mentally active and thoughtful; Earth signs are constructive and practical; Water signs are emotional and have strong feelings.

It also shows the metals and gemstones associated with, or corresponding with, each sign. The correspondence is made when a metal or stone possesses properties that are held in common with a particular sign of the zodiac.

Finally, the table shows the opposite of each star sign – this is the opposite sign in the astrological circle.

Placed	Sign	Symbol	Element	Planet	Metal	Stone	Opposite
1	Aries	Ram	Fire	Mars	Iron	Bloodstone	Libra
2	Taurus	Bull	Earth	Venus	Copper	Sapphire	Scorpio
3	Gemini	Twins	Air	Mercury	Mercury	Tiger's Eye	Sagittarius
4	Cancer	Crab	Water	Moon	Silver	Pearl	Capricorn
5	Leo	Lion	Fire	Sun	Gold	Ruby	Aquarius
6	Virgo	Maiden	Earth	Mercury	Mercury	Sardonyx	Pisces
7	Libra	Scales	Air	Venus	Copper	Sapphire	Aries
8	Scorpio	Scorpion	Water	Pluto	Plutonium	Jasper	Taurus
9	Sagittarius	Archer	Fire	Jupiter	Tin	Topaz	Gemini
10	Capricorn	Goat	Earth	Saturn	Lead	Black Onyx	Cancer
11	Aquarius	Waterbearer	Air	Uranus	Uranium	Amethyst	Leo
12	Pisces	Fishes	Water	Neptune	Tin	Moonstone	Virgo